Nightworks

Other Books by Marvin Bell

Poetry for a Midsummer's Night [1998]

Ardor: The Book of the Dead Man, Vol. 2 [1997]

The Book of the Dead Man [1994]

A Marvin Bell Reader: Selected Poetry and Prose [1994]

Iris of Creation [1990]

New and Selected Poems [1987]

Drawn by Stones, by Earth, by Things That Have Been in the Fire [1984]

Old Snow Just Melting: Essays and Interviews [1983]

Segues: A Correspondence in Poetry (with William Stafford) [1983]

These Green-Going-to-Yellow [1981]

Stars Which See, Stars Which Do Not See [1977]

Residue of Song [1974]

The Escape into You [1971]

A Probable Volume of Dreams [1969]

Things We Dreamt We Died For [1966]

Nightworks

POEMS 1962–2000

Marvin Bell

COPPER CANYON PRESS

Printed in the United States of America.

Cover art: untitled photograph (detail), copyright
Isabelle Rozenbaum/PhotoAlto

Copper Canyon Press is in residence under the auspices of
the Centrum Foundation at Fort Worden State Park in
Port Townsend, Washington. Centrum sponsors artist residencies,
education workshops for Washington State students and teachers,
Blues, Jazz, and Fiddle Tunes Festivals, classical music performances,
and the Port Townsend Writers' Conference.

LIBRARY OF CONGRESS CATALOGING-IN-PUBLICATION DATA
Bell, Marvin.
    Nightworks : poems 1962–2000 / Marvin Bell.
        p.   cm.
    ISBN 1-55659-180-2 (paper edition) / ISBN 1-55659-147-0
(cloth edition)
    I. Title.
PS3552.E52 N54 2000

                                                    00-010283

SECOND EDITION
3 5 7 9 8 3 4 2
FIRST PRINTING

COPPER CANYON PRESS
Post Office Box 271
Port Townsend, Washington 98368
www.coppercanyonpress.org

Acknowledgments

The poems in *Nightworks* were selected from the following collections: *Things We Dreamt We Died For* (The Stone Wall Press, 1966); *A Probable Volume of Dreams* (Atheneum, 1969); *The Escape into You* (Atheneum, 1971); *Residue of Song* (Atheneum, 1974); *Stars Which See, Stars Which Do Not See* (Atheneum, 1977); *These Green-Going-to-Yellow* (Atheneum, 1981); *Drawn by Stones, by Earth, by Things That Have Been in the Fire* (Atheneum, 1984); *New and Selected Poems* (Atheneum, 1987); *Iris of Creation* (Copper Canyon Press, 1990); *A Marvin Bell Reader* (Middlebury College Press/University Press of New England, 1994); *The Book of the Dead Man* (Copper Canyon Press, 1994); *Ardor: The Book of the Dead Man, Vol. 2* (Copper Canyon Press, 1997); and *Poetry for a Midsummer's Night* (Seventy Fourth Street Productions, 1998). Grateful acknowledgment is given to John C. Ross for his musical setting of "After a Line by Theodore Roethke" and to Patricia Staton Thomas for her stage adaptation of "Dead Man" poems, "Life with the Dead Man, or How I Fell for Entropy." Some poems have been slightly revised. An earlier version of "The Book of the Dead Man (#1)" appeared in *Iris of Creation*.

In previous appearances, the poems titled "Sounds of the Resurrected Dead Man's Footsteps" bore numbers indicating the order of composition. They have been renumbered for this collection. "Sounds of the Resurrected Dead Man's Footsteps" poems first appeared in the following books and periodicals:

And What Rough Beast (Ashland Poetry Press, 1999): (#2) Skulls / Skulls; (#3) Beast, Peach and Dance / Angel, Portrait and Breath.

Black Warrior Review: (#7) Odysseus / Inconsolable Love.

The Dickinson Review: (#8) His Knickers, His High Shoes / His Windbreaker, His Watch Cap.

Field: (#9) Exquisite Disembodiment / Apotheosis and Separation; (#17) At the Walking Dunes, Eastern Long Island / Walking in the Drowning Forest.

The Georgia Review: (#12) Today, Tibet / Tomorrow, Tibet; (#13) That Swine Are Intelligent / That Ducks Are Dumb; (#14) Lives of the Whales / Old Whalers Church, Sag Harbor; (#19) Griddle, Grease and Piecrust / Oboe, Drum and Pocket Trumpet.

The Gettysburg Review: (#4) Indeterminate Time / Yes and No; (#6) A Tree in a Window, the Window Itself, and the Mustard-Colored Butter Substitute That Might Be the Sun / Coos Bay; (#10) Dog, Bell and Blossom / Kneecap, Whiskey and Glass; (#21) Less Judgment / Less Self.

The Hampden-Sydney Poetry Review: (#18) One Potato Two / Three Potato Four.

The Iowa Review: (#16) Oneself / One's Other Self.

The Kenyon Review: (#15) Man Burning a Field / Vertigo.

Many Mountains Moving: (#11) Passion / Consolation.

The New Bread Loaf Anthology of Contemporary American Poetry: (#2) Skulls / Skulls.

Poetry: (#20) Shakespeare Expected / Shakespeare Dismissed.

Prairie Schooner: (#2) Skulls / Skulls; (#3) Beast, Peach and Dance / Angel, Portrait and Breath.

Shenandoah: (#1) Baby Hamlet / The Play Within the Play; (#5) Fly, Fleece and Tractor / Syringe, Cloak and Elevator.

Spud Songs (Helicon Nine Editions, 1999): (#18) One Potato Two / Three Potato Four.

Walking in the Footsteps of the Dead Man (Sutton Hoo Press, 2000): (#1) Baby Hamlet / The Play Within the Play; (#5) Fly, Fleece and Tractor / Syringe, Cloak and Elevator; (#11) Passion / Consolation; (#12) Today, Tibet / Tomorrow, Tibet.

Dorothy

Nathan

Jason

Leslie

Colman

Aileen

Contents

Sounds of the Resurrected Dead Man's Footsteps

Sounds of the Resurrected
Dead Man's Footsteps (#1)

1. Baby Hamlet

Be that as it may, it may be that it is as it will be.
His word a sword without a hiss.
Cruelly, the son obliged to sacrifice himself to a feud.
On the Feast of the Angel of Consumption and Death.
We move through time beset by indecision.
Thus, events occur while waiting for the news.
Or stuck in moral neutral.
The Nazis willing to let aid enter the camps if those bringing it
        swore not to help the prisoners escape.
The hopeless pacifism of those who promised.
The Platonic ideal carried to its logical inconclusion.
The heroes those who lied to the Third Reich.
Otherwise, the world stands caught between Hamlet and Ophelia.
Ophelia's dress a dead ringer for beauty.

2. The Play Within the Play

Hamlet a man asked to die now.
Madness to try to make sense of a father's ghost.
To know one lives yet may not.
To imbibe a poison over time — wishing to be, yet consigned.
And the work details, the meager rations, the Motherland.
Destined to clog the machinery of the State with one's body, Nazis
        the masters of whitewash.
Fairy dust rising from lime shoveled into the grave.
Poems and postmortems a struggle with Danish collaboration.
Hamlet a play of ones foreshadowing a time of millions.
Hamlet addressing a skull the poet speaking to the dead.
Bones the bloodless gray of ancient manuscripts.
The eyes marbles clicking in their pockets.
Hamlet done to death with his head in his hands.

Sounds of the Resurrected
Dead Man's Footsteps (#2)

1. Skulls

Oh, said a piece of tree bark in the wind, and the night froze.
One could not have foreseen the stoppage.
I did not foresee it, who had expected a messiah.
No one had yet dared say that he or she was it — target or savior.
In the slippage between time and the turning planet, a buildup of
        dirty grease made movement difficult.
Time slowed down while events accelerated.
The slower the eye moved, the faster events went past.
The raping and pillaging over time became one unending moment.
Nazis, who would always stand for the crimes of culture, clustered in
        public intersections, awaiting deliveries.
The masses would turn in the Jews.
From the officers' quarters could be heard the beautiful Schubert.
And in the camp there was the grieving tenor of the cantor.
The one rose and the other sank.
Today, one can stroll in the footsteps of those who walked single file
        from this life.
Often I stand in the yard at night expecting something.
Something in the breeze one caught a scent of as if a head of hair
        had passed by without a face.
Whatever happens to us from now on, it will come up from the earth.
It will bear the grief of the exterminated, it will lug itself upward.
It will take all of our trucks to carry the bones.
But the profane tattoos have been bled of their blue by the watery
        loam, additives for worms.
Often I stand in the yard with a shovel.

2. Skulls

I am the poet of skulls without why or wherefore.

I didn't ask to be this or that, one way or another, just a young
        man of words.

Words that grew in sandy soil, words that fit scrub trees and
        beach grass.

Sentenced to work alone where there is often no one to talk to.

The poetry of skulls demands complicity of the reader, that the
        reader put words in the skull's mouth.

The reader must put water and beer in the mouth, and music in the
        ears, and fan the air for aromas to enter the nostrils.

The reader must take these lost heads to heart.

The reader must see with the eyes of a skull, comb the missing hair
        of the skull, brush the absent teeth, kiss the lips and find
        the hinge of the tongue.

Yes, like Hamlet, the Jew of Denmark before Shakespeare
        seduced him.

It is the things of the world which rescue us from the degradations
        of the literati.

A work shirt hanging from a nail may be all the honesty we can
        handle.

I am beloved of my hat and coat, enamored of my bed, my troth
        renewed each night that my head makes its impression
        on the pillow.

I am the true paramour of my past, though my wife swoons at
        the snapshots.

Small syringe the doctor left behind to charm the child.

Colorful yarmulke that lifted the High Holy Days.

Sounds of the Resurrected
Dead Man's Footsteps (#3)

1. Beast, Peach and Dance

He couldn't say it or write it or sign it or give it a name.

He was suffering, he was terrible, he had a shape you could see in
the fire.

He blamed the wine, God, the infamous events of Bethlehem.

Each newborn appeared to him in the air, their gorgeous
proportions shaping the swaddling cloth each to each.

On the one hand, he felt the galaxies cooling, the gears clogging and
the old passions frozen into debilitating poses.

On the other hand, it was now April and he had a buzz on because
some seasons are their own nectar.

He could pick out a jacket and tie if he had to.

He could sit without twitching through the outdoor Mozart, the
band shell gleaming like a new star.

Around him, the concertgoers sat tight-lipped, their expectations
rewarded.

Before him, the night took on the sheen of flat glass and he could see
in it the beacons of the town, and the blue-blackness of
space just beyond.

His eyes fixed on a small, fuzzy star among many larger stars.

He became obsessed with this star, certain it was a Jewish star.

He felt that, if he could follow it, it would lead him to the true story
of Jesus.

That night, while Mozart resolved in the air, he began to travel
through time.

His small star would someday pass close to him but not yet.

2. Angel, Portrait and Breath

The hands that were nailed, the ankles that were pierced as if one —
        he had seen such proclamations before, it being common.
The bodies that literally came unglued in the furnace, the bones
        festering in lye — he had seen the piles of coats and
        eyeglasses, there being many.
The same angel who watched over the crucified Jesus passed over the
        cremated Jews, or was that a cloud?
The smokestacks carried away their last breaths.
Then Jesus rose entire to show the power of belief.
The dead Jews disintegrated into earth, air and water to show the
        lasting effects of evil.
He could not give it a name but felt that night as if, whatever it was,
        it lived on a small star, encircled but apart.
Thereafter, ordinary objects displayed a consciousness of the
        presence of men and women.
The blackened pots and ladles of the kitchen appeared changed.
They shone from long years of sustenance, from soups and sauces.
And in the shop he felt it also in the saws and sawhorses, in the
        drop cloths and bent nails, each encrusted with the years.
In this manner, he came to see in common objects the shine of
        the angelic.
The divine and horrific were linked by things and their descendants.
It was possible to see the good and bad in a needle and thread, in a
        pencil and pad, in a spoon, in a shoe.
The cloud appeared to him by day and the little star by night.

Sounds of the Resurrected
Dead Man's Footsteps (#4)

1. Indeterminate Time

I know in a general way what Chagall intended in the sky.
I think he meant "yes."
I think I know the yes he meant and what he meant by it.
Unlike old age, unlike a stone alone in the morning.
If I left, for example, the Army, as soon as I was able.
If I had, for example, the opportunity to stay for twenty years.
In olive drab with a squint beneath the visor.
There are those who can't imagine it, not possible, can't understand.
All of this is yesterday, but also in the future.
I left after less than two years, and every night thereof.
I never took a leave — the job and the money.

2. Yes and No

Chagall and I come from the same stock.
One who chopped off his trigger finger to avoid the Czar's army.
One who never had a childhood so I might.
People fleeing, untethered.
All of them in steerage so none would have to hide.
I am coming down the street that leads to my house.
My Army savings the down payment.
They were surprised by the intelligence test.
It was all just Yes, every answer was Yes.
I knew the right answers were always cruel, just the facts.
The time I had nothing to say to the colonel but Sir.

Sounds of the Resurrected
Dead Man's Footsteps (#5)

1. Fly, Fleece and Tractor

Legs arrayed, a spider observes me from the juncture of wall
          and ceiling.
Little sunspot, unmoved by the rustle of a writer's clothes,
          undisturbed by the passing locomotive saying "Q," "Q."
They all come to passing grief who ride these walls.
They perish by degrees who deny the wolf.
They are ground underfoot who fuss instead of running.
After insect-killing season, there comes the machinery, then the
          corn upstanding and the animals grown to harvest.
Then again the machinery.
He had been indoors, who planned to go outside.

2. Syringe, Cloak and Elevator

In a planting field, a tractor bears down on the evidence.
It does not feel the modernist division of mind and body.
Like liquid within a syringe, some people need a push to go out.
Elsewhere, they who deny evil are covered by goodness and
          must suffer.
Those who cannot go forward and backward must go up and down.
He was farming, who was taken to the hospital.
The long winter was of thunder snow, and the spring cacophony
          was of the wind and the almanac, and the silence is the
          quiet of being watched.
One last late-night toot from the pantheistic locomotive, then
          the owls.

Sounds of the Resurrected
Dead Man's Footsteps (#6)

*I. A Tree in a Window, the Window Itself, and the Mustard-Colored
Butter Substitute That Might Be the Sun*

Then he looked up from the potato fields.
If not for the tree, he might never have noticed the window.
He felt he had been lucky beyond belief, sane past reason, one
        tolerated by time.
Because someone planted a tree.
Because someone with a claw hammer caulked the window.
So anyone can live on the margin, not that it's a plan.
Happiness is optional.
The owl's cluck is the mouse's alarm.
The rat now shivers in sleep who abandoned the boat for
        the boathouse.
You know the way they say, The grass is always greener...?
It was crucial to have seen the otherness of things at hand.
To have pictured the owl clucking, shivering the wood.
To have felt the sun claw away the alarming option of night.
That we will wake in a boathouse on the Styx.
Yet the margarine in the morning seems to emit those solar flares
        that wobble the frequencies.
We try to get the news on the radio, but it's so far away.

2. Coos Bay

The red snapper that was lunch.
The tooth that broke, the arm that creaked, the knee that wobbled.
One half expected the freighter beyond the quay to raise the
        Jolly Roger.
And Moby Dick's our favorite sea lion.
The *whooom whooom* of the foghorn coated the early morning.
Block and tackle sang at sea, and the snapper sang back.
Orion envied Van Allen his mighty belt of stars.
Everything going from one place to another without moving.
Nations afloat in the continental drift.
And he, who thought he saw a tree through a window, saw only
        his mind.
Even then, he was lucky beyond belief, sane past reason.
When there is no sworn millennium, no first year, no tickle of time,
        no end in sight, then he is keen to witness the otherness
        at hand.
The signers of the Declaration of Independence saw something that
        wasn't there.
The owl clucks just to think there might be another field mouse.
Who knows where anything started?
The birthmark caused by his mother's diet of fish.

Sounds of the Resurrected
Dead Man's Footsteps (#7)

1. Odysseus

Some mornings, stepping on shore, the wind relentless, he is sad.
As sad as a siren at the end of its wail.
Sad as the remnant of red thread twisted around the button of
        a mattress.
Her pillow whispers and the bedspread sighs.
Her kiss lingers on his neck though she is not to be turned to.
Her body was the needle that stitched a hull of the blankets and
        made of the waves an ocean.
He wept at the sight of her robe over the chair, and left in the dawn.
Ashore, he sings the song that will immortalize her name.
He speaks the sonnets into which their love is disappearing.
This wind seems a punishment of the air.
The tide line seems the border of a chopped mirror in which one
        can see facets of a pianist fingering the black keys.
Intrigue still kisses the ivy up and down the lattice outside
        her window.
An unfinished diary lies forever bound to the sheen of a bedside
        tabletop.
The ivory statues are cold.

2. Inconsolable Love

The kiss was succulent.

The touch of a pearl between her breasts made a sound so soft it
        had to be imagined.

He muffled his temptation in case he should fail.

His worst dream was of a twilight Ice Age, her pale flesh abused
        by disuse.

At sunrise, pale clams seethe beneath the tide line.

He listens for a language lodged in sand.

A colony of sand fleas chattering, the bones of a horse knocking.

He is ardent to feel what he felt, and he shadowboxes the surf.

Here is a dark washed-up crab carcass of the earth.

And a bleached, unburied shell of the light.

Just so, he knows the measure of her torso by its absence.

They will never again meet in an airy meadow or pasture.

He is Odysseus lashed to a wreck.

The supple wind shifts, like the lace of her dress when she walks.

Sounds of the Resurrected
Dead Man's Footsteps (#8)

1. His Knickers, His High Shoes

Whereas yesterday he made his hand feel the sky, his leg fathom the
        floor, today I remember the child he was without knowing.
That he could have been nineteen forever in regard to his body.
So much the scout, looking back after years of unexplored territory.
Were it not for his propensity for sunstroke.
Due to the hottest days involved, he started as a secret something new.
No surprise that, four years after I met him, he realized I was a
        serious disciple creating the function of a limb.
He was forty-nine at the time of his life's work in the course of a
        two-part performance.
Of which I was not to think too much for several years.
Whether or not it was for other people that he entered work in
        this way.

2. His Windbreaker, His Watch Cap

I was at forty-nine a lifetime of not knowing.
He was, for me, found light.
If he liked to number the days of my childhood, then the fascination
        for me was to work closely from his verbal expression.
So much was he the one I paid attention to.
No surprise that he wore the shreds and tatters from which I had
        long been making one into more than one.
Whether or not he was now me or I was he.
That he could have been, meant layers and layers of material.
Were it not for my propensity for sunstroke.
Ask me again if who I was is who I have become.

Sounds of the Resurrected
Dead Man's Footsteps (#9)

1. Exquisite Disembodiment

He who left a splotch of powder on the bathroom floor has
        checked out.
Whose figure then lay embedded in the grass.
Whose pillow last night lay shattered like an alabaster ruin.
His thumbprint remains on the rim of the glass where the liquor ran
        over his finger and around his tongue.
On the bedside table, a half-eaten pear, the teeth marks still glistening.
The bedsheets limp, the reformed pillows devoid of their impressions.
On the terrace a man and a woman sit drinking coffee as calmly as
        lovers in an elegant sketch.
At the piano, a black wisp of smoke rises from the keys.
He bends to whisper to her, back and forth like a whip hissing.
It is hard to sit with her in the breeze unable to know what she knows.

2. Apotheosis and Separation

Like the kiss of a whip on the sand.
And was it he whose face appeared languidly in the tide pool when
        he looked?
The salt whitening on his cheek a second before being washed away
        by the rain.
Walking in the mist and hearing in the water the sounds of wreckage.
Romantics who rode out on the mirror till it cracked.
Their love ripened while the moon undressed and they sailed.
He thinks of her arms around him, her breasts against his back, and
        one of them asleep.
Her dreams a sea in a temperate zone.
Her one dream a streak of moonlight on the ground where she runs.
The galley closed, and nothing exposed to the air that might spoil.

Sounds of the Resurrected
Dead Man's Footsteps (#10)

1. Dog, Bell and Blossom

Were it not for the pests in the blossoms and the mildew on the sill.
Were it not for the blight that blocked heaven.
Every seven years, every seventeen, every time for the first time.
If it's not the cicadas, it's the millennium or the coming apocalypse.
Decisions made on bridges and high-rise terraces.
Words drowning in a sea of actions.
He belled the cat who liked birds more.
He trimmed his nails so he could drum his fingertips.
Ruby the color of sheep at sunset.
Of course you have to look from a distance.
You have to stick your elbow in the ghost's ribs to get an answer.
You have to root around in the ashes like a dog.
It's a kind of a priori salvation to be a juicy mango in the sun.
Were it not for the distillation.
Were it not for the decomposition.

2. Kneecap, Whiskey and Glass

Other than the pain in his knees, the walk down the steps is a snap.
Water, his whiskey.
His hand cut by glass, the blood scarlet, crimson, cherry on top,
      brown when left, black when dry.
Light can't get through him the way it once did.
They say old bones are light bones, but only when raised.
The whites of his eyes alive now with transport.
He thinks he has become a cosmos of parts flying from the center
      at reckless speed.
But it was this way all along, a grain that grew because it knew
      how to.
To think he once lifted the parts of Stonehenge.
How little he knew of the force of nature, just some numbers.
Environment the conscious, heredity the unconscious.
Surprised to discover that uphill was the easy part.
A rose winks among the thorns.
A faint voice breaks the silence to say hush.
Unless it be that a hair-raising wind is just about to come through.

Sounds of the Resurrected
Dead Man's Footsteps (#11)

1. Passion

Out looking for a new blue sky, and the ground soaked.
The worms drowning in the wet air, and the last of the lightning
         spreads sheets in the east.
We have come into a new season with old concerns.
That there will be the lacy filigree of new buds before long, and
         that time will be long but our pleasures soon.
That we should live to see it and hear it when the crickets
         buzz again.
We bow before the least objects, grateful for their loyalty.
Then comes the rain and the ice pellets on the roof.
How there arrived last evening the timelessness, the bottomlessness,
         the rush of air into the lungs that bears the sleeper upward
         in panic.
That never in youth felt so carried away.
I do not believe in the instant but in the place.
Dusk came and a black sky and I was made by time to go indoors.
Let me, I said, and took a breath, and was startled awake like one
         who had overslept.

2. Consolation

Books stowed for forty years now weigh less.
It might be Montaigne, it might be Mill, it might be Zane Grey.
Their yellowed pages, skins toxic and tawny from long
        imprisonment.
The smell of their long-shelved wraps and bindings, delicate
        rubbings of fibers risen from the spines.
He in panic could do worse than an armchair in the window and a
        cheap book from an easier time.
With an arm over the chair back where it seems to passersby an eerie
        chunk of late night.
And the only light in the house thrown over his shoulder to fix
        whatever may be there in his lap, a book or a skull.

Sounds of the Resurrected
Dead Man's Footsteps (#12)

1. Today, Tibet

One day I have fifteen minutes to stop the ruination.
Today, Tibet.
Other places, other days, but today Tibet.
This thin air makes me dizzy.
I breathe not deeply but partially, and I slip on the sleety
        condensation.
Bones keep at this altitude.
Mountains top the clouds and I have come with the lowdown.
Prayer wheels and a hollow wind at this altitude.
Now fifteen minutes of the ghostly as I tour the rim of a rice bowl.
They are clothed in shadow who breathe deeply and sit censored in
        the monasteries.
What low chant, what undertone of peace, what karmic rumor can
        sweep away an army?
Necessary to show them calm targets.
Necessary to suffer the hollow wind to moan, the bones to clack and
        a stench to settle in the rice.
One day I have fifteen minutes on the front page.
Other places, other days, but today Tibet.

2. Tomorrow, Tibet

Yesterday, a people.
Tomorrow, an obit, a footnote, an explanation.
Yesterday, an earthen water vessel.
Today, the chipped, the shattered, the missing, the buried.
Those high-pointed hats to top the stars.
Those spinning tapestries of prayer, now shreds.
Tatters that thread the wind with fringe, gut, remembrance of
        things past.
Coins for Hamlet to take up alms.
I don't want to hear this, chants that catch in the throat.
I don't want to see this, like a dead fox mounted on a barbed-wire
        fence.
Travel the back country, it's Tibet.
Fuss a little, make good time, see the sights, it's Tibet.
Tibet the land that was, is, and shall remain... unwritten.
The wind exiled, the clouds scattered, a people sacked.
How shall we move mountains when Tibet disappears in thin air?

Sounds of the Resurrected
Dead Man's Footsteps (#13)

1. That Swine Are Intelligent

Was three hundred pounds and hard to turn over.
The stubby legs locked, askew, and the feet biting the ground.
The refusal.
The ice pick through the keyhole of the throat.
The artery unlocked.
Up rose the red fountain and fell back by stages.
The pig deflated, the calm overcoming, the silence broken.
Farm boys name them.
They come when called, have been known to throw the switch.
The electric fence goes down, and no one around but a pig.

2. That Ducks Are Dumb

Their paddle-wheel effort under the surface.
The short necks that beat the swans to the bread.
Their tendency to trample one another for food.
And the eggs of no concern.
Lacking the Boy Scout ability of the gull, the heft of the goose.
Jealous of others but made to flock together.
Then they rise up in a vee to look elsewhere.
Stretching the summer.
Easily decoyed, prey to the group, joined in cacophony.
Ponderous mudders, oblivious to the shoreline.

Sounds of the Resurrected
Dead Man's Footsteps (#14)

1. Lives of the Whales

No larger captive mammal.
Oh but you should see one pitch in the wake.
To have risen from the sea empirical, its song Scriabin a temple.
Its song the quiver of a fork, its song a high nest of bees.
Its infinite longing, its heavy body, its grief.
The pod moving like a constellation past the land.
Body of my body beyond my body.
Loaves of sea bread we commend to you.
The frozen compasses of hulks that failed to cross.
You at a safe distance.
Your blatant disregard of proportion.

2. Old Whalers Church, Sag Harbor

Whose proportion?
Begins spotty moisture, then wind-driven shards.
Whalers Church weather, clapboard days.
Madmen believe the Devil inhabits a whale, swelling it.
Jonah, every man's fear.
Who elsewhere took buffalo for food and warmth.
Here took whales, there being access and harbor.
The oil a rich bonus.
The difficulty seeing oneself so increased.
Therefore, the taut gut strings of harpoon talk.
The annals of marine literature in thankful service to God.

Sounds of the Resurrected
Dead Man's Footsteps (#15)

1. Man Burning a Field

The growth underfoot, the amputated remains.
Heracleitus watches the change from earth to air by way of fire.
He observes from a distance called "time."
The merely molecular dispersion of that which was a Greek.
The stubble in smoke casts a dark net.
The dry stumps rise, disperse and settle back into the earth.
He has work to do, the igniter of next season, the flame thrower.
His silhouette follows and frightens the man with the hoe.
His hand afire a version of the reaper with his scythe.
Before the burning, we were innocent amidst the grain.
Afterward, we had knowledge of intention, we had memory.
No Eden, no kingdom come, no nirvana.
This charred dust in limbo, this sacrificial gulp of air.
Literally takes your breath away.

2. Vertigo

He couldn't walk across the hanging bridge a second time.
Became one of those drivers nervous on a span.
Images of others driven over lying on the car floor.
Fear of burying one's head in the sand.
Placing furniture in front of balcony doors in hotels.
A sudden fear of sleepwalking for the first time.
That he should die before he wakes.
No Eden, no kingdom come, no nirvana.
And the drivers oblivious surmounting the archway.
The girders swaying, sense of a bed sinking.
This nightly eternity without doors.
A leap of no look.
A stepping into the same river once.
An egg that was dropped from a rooftop to see what.

Sounds of the Resurrected
Dead Man's Footsteps (#16)

1. Oneself

A story told over the shoulder, a memory foreign to the touch.
A visitation, a meteor or the idea of a meteor.
Not having had a key at that age, or a voice from outside.
But there were heroes up the road, and a bicycle.
He was myself and can't use all the words.
It was often after midnight in those days, with a heart on one's
        sleeve and dreams under one's hat.
Tiers of identity, activity badges, certificates of merit.
A lopsided planet, in that he was not another person.
This disadvantage, not being another, meant constant defeat.
So it was necessary to eat his words.
Our eagle was a gull.
Our orchards were the potato fields.

2. One's Other Self

I want to understand.
It was a town where watermarks meant the moon.
An island where the tides took men's lives.
A quarry was our Grand Canyon.
We lived for the end of the line, the tip of the peninsula, the
        deserted beach.
And a girlfriend, we lived for someone to live for.
So a book here and a book there, and then you're talking
        to yourself.
I walked in the gas of the dead fish and the algae.
I failed neatness and penmanship.
I learned that language can think for itself.
I needed to stop myself from thinking everything at once.
Our ocean was the ocean, but our England was just tea.

Sounds of the Resurrected Dead Man's Footsteps (#17)

1. At the Walking Dunes, Eastern Long Island

That a bent piece of straw made a circle in the sand.
That it represents the true direction of the wind.
Beach grass, tousled phragmite.
Bone-white dishes, scoops and bowls, glaring without seeing.
An accordion of creases on the downhill, sand drapery.
The cranberry bushes biting down to survive.
And the wind's needlework athwart the eyeless Atlantic.
And the earless roaring in the shape of a sphere.
A baritone wind, tuned to the breath of the clouds.
Pushing sand that made a hilly prison of time.
For wind and water both move inland.
Abrading scrub — the stunted, the dwarfed, the bantam.
A fine sandpaper, an eraser as wide as the horizon.
Itself made of galaxies, billions against the grain.
Sand: the mortal infinitude of a single rock.

2. *Walking in the Drowning Forest*

Pitch pine, thirty-five-foot oaks to their necks in sand.
That the ocean signals the lighthouse.
Gull feathers call to the fox that left them behind.
Impressions of deer feet, dog feet and gull claws.
The piping plover in seclusion.
Somewhere the blind owl to be healed at sunset.
Here is artistry beyond self-flattery.
A rootworks wiser than the ball of yarn we call the brain.
A mindless, eyeless, earless skin-sense.
To which the crab comes sideways.
With which the sunken ship shares its secrets.
From which no harness can protect one, nor anchor fix one.
He knows, who has paddled an hour with one oar.
He knows, who has worn the whitecaps.
Who has slipped from the ferry or leaped from the bridge.
To be spoken of, though no one knows.

Sounds of the Resurrected
Dead Man's Footsteps (#18)

1. One Potato Two

Wrong for the early robin still the potato buries its head in the dirt.
Eyes that cannot see.
1 potato 2 potato a counting game when the choice doesn't matter.
Spotty moisture, overcast, grayness of time immemorial they
        grow in.
Hapless underground severance from light.
Some blight, big bins of why bother if this is the crop you get.
City folk pay big for potato lands.
Acres rank with heavy potato meat.
Fruit of the dirt, bodies bound by gravity.
Face like a potato, chest like a potato, belly like a potato.
Never had a potato a wing.

2. Three Potato Four

All representation is neutral.
Thinking the subject suffered, you suffered.
Bagging the potatoes, you strained a back better suited to crawling.
The worm fitter for tuber life.
Knots in the furrows.
Potato brandy a flat water scraped from the peel.
You are this and these, bulb without light, black hole encrusted.
One's intention to be better than one's roots a betrayal.
Soup and stew, potions to throw cool water on the crop.
Haunted by what it might have been.
In the shadow, a ghost potato where one was taken.

Sounds of the Resurrected
Dead Man's Footsteps (#19)

1. Griddle, Grease and Piecrust

Fry cook a skill one could always land a job with, go live anywhere.
Lacking a chef's bravado, unbowed before desserts.
Postman also a good career, but sidewalks are worse on the body.
Too early to blink, I take a stool at the counter with the postman
        and the policeman.
We share a benign disinterest in the day, who loved too late
        the night.
Beeped from bed, called to account, the cradle rocked, the
        bough broken.
Our fry cook jacks up the heat till the grease pops.
There's no blemish on bacon, no spot in the eggs that will not cook.
There's nothing black in a potato that can't be fried.
A secret in the batter makes it better.
And the piecrusts in this place could make up for breakfast.
If you missed it, that is.
Meanwhile, the special is fry bread and blasphemy.
And coffee and cakes and bravura and borscht.

2. Oboe, Drum and Pocket Trumpet

All the notes are downwind.
The bravado of the brass, the beatitude of the high reeds.
The bovine tympani.
And the little trumpet in a bag, all curled up on itself.
Sometimes it looks like an inner organ, an esophagus — all the
        little pipes.
And the trombone a kind of rubber hose.
That there could have been music not known to be music.
That it could be played directly on the body: with reeds and
        mouthpieces, and percussive spoons.
Our lungs the bellows blowing hot and cool.
Rim shots probably a lucky mistake in the beginning.
He thinks so, who has been bushwhacked by a rim shot, blasted by
        overblown brasses, or just lay in bed listening to static.
One is always downwind from the music.
One always believes it began elsewhere and arrived here later.
The pocket trumpet a way to take it with you.

Sounds of the Resurrected
Dead Man's Footsteps (#20)

1. Shakespeare Expected

William Shakespeare of an actual presence.
His knee sore from kneeling, his teeth chattering, his wrap wet and
        gritty from the dirty rain.
I take a front seat at the rehearsal where he is expected.
Hamlet has shown, his hand already cupped to hold a skull.
Ophelia presses out her dress, still damp from having been worn
        under her coat.
And Shakespeare is trudging, trudging, toward the theater.
Trying to get in the mood in this weather is like trying to play a
        piano with mittens.
The day is too thickly about one.
The crowd sees in his dramas the debris of an exhausted court.
While his patrons, addicted to bouquets, believe them to be the
        consummate valediction of their lively personalities.
Here he comes now, a bard in sheep's clothing.
At the stage door, he steps out of his time and into the future.
I can see now that Ophelia will drown in her beauty before she dies.
That Hamlet will kill himself first in word, then in deed.

2. Shakespeare Dismissed

I can't say why he thinks himself Shakespeare at the window.
I can't explain his predilection for iambics and balconies.
He has fallen on his sword, he has nothing.
The gangrenous covers of old books stick together on the shelves.
People have memorized his sonnets for their own reasons.
Why have I not spoken to him?
What do you think he thinks about, this old derelict of words?
This overgrown boy who cannot let go of a lump of coal.
Who has broken the balsa airplane.
And now dons a canvas coat to make his way to the theater in
      the rain.
And a cap, and sunglasses in the winter.
I swear, trying to get in the right mood still means falling on
      one's sword.
The backslapping buffoonery, the sublimity of tragedy — he has the
      bruises and the scars, and the sinkholes of infection.
Here he is now, stepping around the shards of a mirror the lead
      actress threw across the stage when she thought he was
      not coming.

Sounds of the Resurrected
Dead Man's Footsteps (#21)

1. Less Judgment

Less judgment is one of those things.
I am following an invisible star.
It could be related to shadow, but it isn't shadow.
It could be ignorance, which it is.
It could be myself underneath the scars, the epistles.
One eye closed, the other winking.
The last light blinking in the evergreens.
On the day we turned back the clocks it got dark.
I sit in the dark while the moon changes its coat.

2. Less Self

Throwing your voice is one of those things also.
They think it's you when it's not you.
They certainly thought it was me.
I was there when the one they thought me said yes.
And no.
I send my voice out under cover of darkness.
It is widely assumed that winter makes the pine tree stronger.
The greenest hours are those after midnight.
Green remains.

Things We Dreamt We Died For

1966

We live in an occupied country, misunderstood;
justice will take us millions of intricate moves.

WILLIAM STAFFORD

The Hole in the Sea

It's there
in the hole of the sea
where the solid truth lies,
written and bottled,
and guarded by limp-
winged angels —
one word under glass,
magnified by longing
and by the light tricks
of the moving man
in the moon.
Nights, that word shows,
up from the bottle,
up through the water,
up from the imaginable.
So that all who cannot
imagine, but yearn toward,
the word in the water,
finding it smaller
in the hole in the sea,
rest there. If no one
has drowned quite
in the hole of the sea,
that is a point
for theology. "Blame God
when the waters part,"
say sailors and Hebrews;
blame God, who writes us,
from His holy solution,
not to be sunk,
though all our vessels

convey black messages
of the end of the world.
So goes the story,
the storybook story, so goes
the saleable story:
Courage is in that bottle,
the driest thing there is.

Treetops

My father moves through the South hunting duck.
It is warm, he has appeared
like a ship, surfacing, where he floats, face up,
through the ducklands. Over the tops
of trees, duck will come, and he strains
not to miss seeing the first of each flock,
although it will be impossible to shoot one
from such an angle, face up like that
in a floating coffin where the lid obstructs
half a whole view, if he has a gun.
Afterlives are full of such hardships.

One meets, for example, in one's sinlessness,
high water and our faithlessness,
so the dead wonder if they are imagined
but they are not quite.

How could they know we know
when the earth shifts deceptively
to set forth ancestors to such pursuits?
My father will be asking, Is this fitting?
And I think so — I, who, with the others,
coming on the afterlife after the fact
in a dream, in a probable volume, in a
probable volume of dreams, think so.

What Songs the Soldiers Sang

Those with few images, lyrics
in which doing and undoing
prevailed, there were conclusions
and many epithets.
To hell with what it might look like!
The idea of breakfast, to take one
example, was a favorite
in the evenings. Also,
the way fields shut down,
and the weight of the equipment.
In choruses full of objects
nothing civilian moved
but loud young men bent on silence
and backbreaking labors.
It was natural to welcome them
with triumphal marches.
Many would return in halves.
The songs, too, about their singing, are lies.
The truth is that some songs were obscene
and that there were no words for others.

Things We Dreamt We Died For

Flags of all sorts.
The literary life.
Each time we dreamt we'd done
the gentlemanly thing,
covering our causes
in closets full of bones
to remove ourselves forever
from dearest possibilities,
the old weapons re-injured us,
the old armies conscripted us,
and we gave in to getting even,
a little less like us
if a lot less like others.
Many, thus, gained fame
in the way of great plunderers,
retiring to the university
to cultivate grand plunder-gardens
in the service of literature,
the young and no more wars.
Their continuing tributes
make them our greatest saviors,
whose many fortunes are followed
by the many who have not one.

The Condition

The darkness within me is growing.
I am turned out.

Thought feeds on it
even as the body is eaten.

Its goodness is without a face.
But it convinces me to look.

It can fade from now until doomsday.
It will not fade.

In the night I see it shining,
like a thing seen.

My Hate

My hate is like ripe fruit
from an orchard, which is mine.

I sink my teeth into it.
I nurse on its odd shapes.

I have grafted every new variety,
walked in my bare feet,

rotting and detached,
on the fallen ones.

Vicious circle. Unfriendly act.
I am eating the whole world.

In the caves of my ill will
I must be stopped.

The Admission

If you love me,
say so.
Snow piles; bridges burn
behind me; I
imagine
that I am alone
and have not
turned toward you so
before. I forget
openings I had not thought of
turning toward,
to tell you, and to tell you
to tell me.
The surroundings affect us;
it is a cause
for love
that you call it
something logical,
taking pleasure in
our finding
ourselves here.
Tell me landscapes
are frames of mind.
I believe words have meaning.
No gift will do.
Tell me what it means
to you.

Walking Thoughts

The sidewalk is growing soft. I am growing soft.
Absence is a principle, a silence wholly.
If the moon fell, there would be no use for it.

What do we mean by "a killing effort"?
Back there, back there the darkness waits.
Everything we know is a circle.

In a dumb country, the one way is everyone's.
And something has a chance in such a land.
Is my last friend ahead under that light?

I walk on, and watchdogs bark crossly.
The other sidewalk is softening also.
It lets me down with curious consistency.

Settling for the average of full and empty
I turn toward home, begin to hurry in the dark,
have talked myself into going back once more.

The Israeli Navy

The Israeli Navy,
sailing to the end of the world,
stocked with grain
and books black with God's verse,
turned back,
rather than sail on the Sabbath.
Six days, was the consensus,
was enough for anyone.

So the world, it was concluded,
was three days wide
in each direction,
allowing three days back.
And Saturdays were given over
to keeping close,
while Sundays the Navy,
all decked out in white
and many-colored skullcaps,
would sail furiously,
trying to go off the deep end.

Yo-ho-ho, would say the sailors,
for six days.
While on the shore their women moaned.

For years, their boats were slow,
and all show.
And they turned into families
on the only land they knew.

A Probable Volume of Dreams

1969

Dumplings in a dream
are not dumplings, but a dream.

YIDDISH PROVERB

Give Back, Give Back

If I married him for length,
none was so little so long.
How think to explain it? —
Words I have known are now his,
his weight rests under my pillow,
I have nothing for floating.

My children are of groceries,
and not of love. None
has fallen for years, none come crying,
as if the middle years were trying
to break me of my light warping.
I am not so lucky for looking.

On the white sheet of his will
my children inherited
the objects of original pleasure, his
for which I gave up pleasure,
for pleasure, in pleasure, to pleasure.
I am the lot of him, as is my wont.

Yet have wanted to wear the ring of him,
hear it and recreate it.
Into the nights those marriages go
to which woman is bound to be used.
All over I hear the breathing pause
at the long entrance of the children.

The Parents of Psychotic Children

They renounce the very idea
of information, they are enamored
of the notion of the white tablet.
Their babies were outrageously beautiful
objects exploding their lives,
moving without compensation
because of them to worlds without them.
They believe they were presented
inadequate safeguards, faulty retribution,
and a concerted retirement into crime
of the many intent on their injury.
No two can agree on the miraculous
by which they were afflicted,
but with economy overcome
their fears of the worst. Their children, alas,
request nothing. And the far-fetched doctors,
out of touch with the serious truth,
are just practical and do not sing,
like the crazy birds, to their offspring.

A Picture of Soldiers

They are doughboys, of doughboy bearing,
shot in the thick-soled brown shoes of trainees,
the high necks and wide brims to be foregone,
and the camp and company of that lost peace.

Here they affected their final rank and file,
from which they recovered to western fronts
to short the batteries of the Kaiser
and oppose the shock waves of his troopers.

They advanced without water, with inadequate
supplies, they lost their weapons but drove on,
when they lost their arms they went without them,
and then without feet and without stomachs.

They dug into the Argonne, buried Belleau Wood,
planted the trenches of forests, seeded their faults;
they lay down at their funerals in those forests,
leaving issue and rations to remainder,

and this rifle-long photo for my study,
in which these soldiers-to-end-all-soldiers
give up their fathering, give to the living
the next invention, the next impossible President.

The Extermination of the Jews

A thousand years from now
they will be remembered as heroes.
A thousand years from now
they will still be promised their past.

Objects of beauty notwithstanding,
once more they will appear
for their ruin, seeking a purse,
hard bread or a heavy weapon

for those who must survive,
but no one shall survive.
We who have not forgotten,
our children shall outremember:

their victims' pious chanting —
last wishes, last Yiddish, last dreaming —
were defeats with which the Gestapo
continues ceasing and ceasing.

Water, Winter, Fire

In the little light of dawn
the mercantile ships of Rome
slide into the breakers.
A rain of waves will hide them
forever beneath our dream.
We have always known of
the buried life, of these sources
of treasure, and of the washing —
the washing we have known.

———

Suddenly, where leaves were,
there is nothing. The seasons
have shifted above us
in an indistinct rustle —
frozen, finally, to silence.
We had always suspected
the dying of all fruit,
and the likelihood of turning
poisonous during the night.

———

Now that building, which has burned
so often, is burning again.
Our books and papers are rising
irretrievably into the heavens.
Heavier things are up and falling,
for which there can be no helping.
We have dreamt in this life before:
now, suddenly, the air is burning;
now it is useless to be home.

Our Subject Death

She told me to tell you not to worry.
Why bother, she said, looking for trouble?
The love of a woman is a course of instruction
with which, she said, you ought to begin.

I did the best I could without being polite.
She was a wheel on my chest, a giant
flightless bird, circling me for attention,
indescribably graceful and even friendly.

So that I knew the pressure was building
to make love to her, and I didn't want to die.
Love, says the husband, what ruin do you
lie in? Love, she says, we are both in one grave.

But the dead are not dead. You can still see them,
standing still. Nothing had changed. Still,
I knew she was my chances, my angel,
humped and struggling, and good for her.

The Escape into You

1971

Love is too young to know what conscience is,
Yet who knows not conscience is born of love?

SHAKESPEARE, SONNET 151

A Biography

Poetry cripples. *Tempus fugit.*
Have removed from the lit'ry wars
the hand of a gentleman in quill,
the blackberry ink mixed with tears,
who sought the ingratitude of his day
as a sculptor, clay or an alchemist, brass.

Poet or poem? Life or art?
He cared for his judgments in their prisons,
he likened himself to a convict,
he lifted his vision to the window,
he dug for the treasures of light,
he entered the solitary's tunnel.

Women he loved he surrendered,
as leaf falls for the love of leaf.
Felons he insulted and readers perverted.
In the cave of the senseless, it all fit:
the thin shafts the stars shone down
could not lighten his life at hard labor.

I Adore You (1960)

What to include? — I borrowed money
from you, rubber bands, like
a rubber band space in your bed, we
banded together. Turned out, forever.
Lust piece, collar and elastic,
I'm glad I was up to participate.

I took time off from work, wife
on the way out, took to you candy
flowers, bittersweet grounds for mid-
morning Mexican divorce stemming
adultery from. Living conditions improved
because receptive to my advances.

In all those pastorals, teetering sheep,
when the wooden lover stubs his
badly extended heart wanting mother.
Not us. Though my father was just dead,
Mother thought you an angel:
down from heaven, up for grabs.

Honi Soit Qui Mal Y Pense

*Meta*physical, not pornography,
to say we balanced each other.
Some thought it bad to exercise
unless trying to have children.
If we had a thousand, it wouldn't
be enough but just crowded.

On a lonely isle, you are
my idea. In a slow dream of going
across China, you are company.
But still I don't love you
because I have no choice.
I love your voice

saying nothing but moans,
no eyes, no moons: pushing the black
back by the virtues of your sex,
which are those parts of you —
heart but one, and that figurative —
I enter into I love.

Rescue, Rescue

I need you like a sailor needs
his hardtack, I have floundered
far from shore away from paradise,
I need you to cut my teeth on.
It's not easy to let you loose,
not to set you up so I'll need you.

I need you when the boat rolls,
when the mast we thought an arrow
snaps; I swim like a stone.
If you're free, I'm over here,
and over here!, and over here!
The better you swim, the more I drown.

I have worried if the lungs can survive
these extra washings, if the heart
won't wrinkle and the hands retract.
What I've given I wouldn't take back.
I wanted something perfect; without me,
the rescues succeed without regrets.

Your Shakespeare

If I am sentenced not to talk to you,
and you are sentenced not to talk to me,
then we wear the clothes of the desert
serving that sentence, we are the leaves
trampled underfoot, not even fit to be
ground in for food, then we are the snow.

If you are not what I take you to be,
and I am not what you take me to be,
then we are the glass the bridegroom smashes,
the lost tribes underfoot, no one sees,
no one can speak to us, in such seas we
drift in we cannot be saved, we are the rain.

If I am unable to help myself,
and you are unable to help yourself,
then anything will happen but nothing follows,
we eat constantly but nothing satisfies.
We live, finally, on the simplest notions:
bits of glass in the head's reticent weather.

We Have Known

We have known such joy as a child knows.
My sons, in whom everything rests,
know that there were those who were deeply
in love, and who asked you in,
and who did not claim a tree of thoughts
like family branches would sustain you.

My sons, in whom I am well pleased,
you will learn that a man is not a child,
and there is that which a woman cannot bear,
but as deep wounds for which you may hate
me, who must live in you a long time,
coursing abrasively in the murky passages.

These poems, also, are such and such passages
as I have had to leave you. If very little
can pass through them, know that I did,
and made them, and finally did not need them.
We have known such joys as a child knows,
and will not survive, though you have them.

American Poets

Vision doesn't mean anything real
for most of them. They dance
beautifully way out on the thin limbs
at the top of the family tree,
which we admired for
its solid trunk and unseen roots

we know go back to other countries
where "God help us" was a prayer
one planted like a seed, staking everything
on labor, luck and no concessions.
All of us remember the rain that year
which exhausted the Czar and the Bolsheviks.

Hungry, wet, not yet sick of ourselves,
we escaped by parting the waters;
we brought this black bread to live on,
and extra enough for a child.
That bread didn't grow on trees.
We multiplied, but we didn't reproduce.

Song of Social Despair

Ethics without faith, excuse me,
is the butter and not the bread.
You can't nourish them all, the dead
pile up at the hospital doors.
And even they are not so numerous
as the mothers come in maternity.

The Provider knows his faults —
love of architecture and repair —
but will not fall into them for long:
he can't afford the adolescent luxury,
the fellowship of the future
looks greedily toward his family.

The black keys fit black cylinders
in the locks in holes in the night.
He had a skeleton key once,
a rubber arm and complete confidence.
Now, as head of the family, he is
inevitably on the wrong side looking out.

Getting Lost in Nazi Germany

You do not move about, but try
to maintain your position. Would you eat
the fruit of the corpses? — You would.
Your friends are the points of a star
now a golden, unattainable "elsewhere"
because there is no elsewhere for a Jew.

Men have closed their daughters to you,
and now the borders like neat hairlines
limiting your ideas to hatred and escape.
This way, they have already begun
the experiments with your brain —
later to be quartered and posted.

Cremation of what remains?
In a dream like this one, a weathered face
will drive you off under a load of hay
at the very moment the Commandant calls.
You could swear the voice you hear is kind,
calling you home, little Jewboy in alarm.

Our Romance

The road is narrow which leads to that house
we have lived in and then eaten like candy.
These were the stories we digested,
and no wonder. The roof was sweet,
the chimney was gum, the mortar was butter,
the end was in sight.

We were the children. We came home at night
to a big bed near a bright light,
and someone bigger just down the hall.
The owls were wise, but we were knowing,
the dark wasn't coming up from downstairs
so fast we couldn't sleep through it.

The children's song would cut its throat;
our hearts, soil our sleeves; yet
how could we know? We were tidy and various,
like jars of preserves in a row:
we saved the children, playing parents;
and saved the parents, being children.

Obsessive

It could be a clip, it could be a comb;
it could be your mother, coming home.
It could be a rooster; perhaps it's a comb;
it could be your father, coming home.
It could be a paper; it could be a pin.
It could be your childhood, sinking in.

The toys give off the nervousness of age.
It's useless pretending they aren't finished:
faces faded, unable to stand,
buttons lost down the drain during baths.
Those were the days we loved down there,
the soap disappearing as the water spoke,

saying, it could be a wheel, maybe a pipe;
it could be your father, taking his nap.
Legs propped straight, the head tilted back;
the end was near when he could keep track.
It could be the first one; it could be the second;
the father of a friend just sickened and sickened.

The Answer

I give the black pit dream's head,
not fearing to hit bottom, to the water
I offer my head like a stone,
just as my tongue enters silence
a thick air collects in both ears,
and then I'm in heaven like a piece of dirt.

What did we think we came to?
A mountain? A molehill? A farm? A well?
Well, we are a little bit of gold after all,
and a small share of lumber and weed.
You could stand outside the owner's gates
for days and yell to cause nothing.

He's hardly ever home. Where he is,
the owl is derisive, and the cow sad.
The bird is too heavy to fly, the fish
too bloated to swim, and men like us,
drowning in words and dreams, thrash wildly
to build up the answer.

What Lasts

So help me, Love, you and I.
Paper into pulp, and our words last
as ashes to cool the sun.
The pen lasts in stories by the fire,
the ink bubbles, the word is cremated
and spreads dumbly as in our lungs.

I wanted to speak it now. And how
the explosive sound of the lungs,
collapsing as they give back air —
we have had that energy, burning.
We have been at the throat of the world.
We have had a lifetime.

I concede to that blue flower, the sky,
a more than passing moral guidance.
Because light flashes, dies, flashes,
some sing the rhapsody of the liver.
Yet what the symbol is to the flower
the flower itself is to something or other.

Constant Feelings

Some acts I could never, not
forthrightly, not by flanking
you, accomplish, like that bridge
the poet tried to put in his poem
to be put in his pocket (another
became a bearskin, already shed).

I wanted to harp on that bridge,
of course to be that bluebottle, corn-
flower, the lobed leaves of the sassafras.
Naturally I hoped the coat of my arms
would, when I reached for you, spin off,
revealing the new skin of a purer animal.

I think I shall always love you.
When I enter your skin, I am closer
to bear, bridge, bush and that tree
which, granting the lovers shade,
will be my veins round yours: many loves
which are lives, but do not depend on lives.

The Willing

I am not yet ready to die inside,
while the ash founds a society of its own
rooted in the clean dirt, while
the berry tree signals its neighborliness
and the weeping willow says "forgive."

Mister of the chapel, Mister of the steeple,
who says go there when the road is a ladder?
I have to take that promise myself
which ended for so many without flowering
and sit the branches and buds through

storm of birth, whipping of circumstance,
lacerations like birthdays in the garden.
Surely foliage needs this beating of foliage
to aspire to: the winds effacing the trees,
the open spaces up ahead pleasing danger.

Put Back the Dark

Let's not stop in cold, in drought,
but blanket and seed our own bed.
We'll be a long time dead.
We walk now on stilts, on dagger heels,
through the howling of impatience
and the ailing imprisoned.

We walk now through the jails,
nothing to provide, a notion of being
free leading us from these helpless,
away from ambition and vanity,
toward the comfort of solitude
like a tree living two-thirds in death.

There is nothing left to resist
where there is nothing irresistible.
So these poor cities fade from vision
not maniacally but as an old memory
which was not important to that dream
when your hand into mine put back the dark.

Song: The Organic Years

Love, if nothing solid rises like wood
above this scratching, this waxen cane
of a tree, if nothing from this trunk
unflowers after long reaching, if finally
the leaf relaxes its bodily processes,
at least we had a hand out to help it.

Also, you have carried me far on your
way into the earth, in the prophetic
imagery of your tunnels I was satisfied,
and in your lovely arms I lay weeping
the truth. If belief doesn't make up
for the long argument of life, still

we made up with what was natural. Now,
from the long, blind alleys of learning,
and in the winter of metaphor, our arms
reach like branches toward the light, our
roots go down to clear water, our fingers,
so long counted on, are not dry yet.

Residue of Song

1974

If you can't get up, get down;
if you can't get across, get across.

YIDDISH PROVERB

Study of the Letter A

A fine A reaches from the soft center
of the skull of a man to either side
of his chin and crosses his face at
the eyes, just as the bridge of the nose
runs the eye of the listener
from eyes to mouth and back again.
The speaker's face itself describes
a square from chin to hair and ear to ear.

The page on which the A appears
in turn's a magic square, undescribed,
neither Satanic nor Diabolic,
like chess in Moscow. Or like ancient
Wisdom, seated squarely on square stone,
while Fortune from a round seat was pleased
this way or that way but never one way.
Some people we will come to are like this.

For now consider the structure of
the fossil sponge: like monkey bars.
Or certain Hittite characters, or semaphores.
The square, pure form of complete idea,
wards off plagues and catches our colds.
We will not see many people in the square.
No deity and no human being lives in this place,
except one woman chosen by the god.

Aristotle

He put in their places as much as he had time for,
and though the word for this is missing
in its entirety we know he knew how it feels
when the hurt and humiliation defeat
guts and gravity to come up out of us
shouting about art instead of murder and giving
to pain the high-sounding name of "tragedy" —
which is a fall from a high place by a weak
sister; i.e., you can jump from a skyscraper
and learn nothing from doing.

Origin of Dreams

Out from muted bee-sounds and musketry
(the hard works of our ears, dissembling),
under steeply-held birds (in that air
the mind draws of our laid breathing),
out from light dust and the retinal gray,
your face as in your forties appears
as if to be pictured, and will not go away.

I have shut up all my cameras, really,
Father, and thought I did not speak to you,
since you are dead. But you last;
are proved in the distance of a wrist.
Your face in dreams sends a crinkly static
and seems, in its mica- or leaf-like texture,
the nightworks of the viscera.

But feeling's not fancy, fancying you.
I don't forget you, or give stinks for thanks.
I think I think the bed's a balcony,
until we sleep. Then our good intentions
lower us to the dead, where we live.
I think that light's a sheet for the days,
which we lose. Then we go looking.

Father and Russia

I see you by thin, flighty apple trees,
picking fruit out of the branched air,
find you in a hand of ice, of which one-third
only appears to welcome but forbid at once.
No, it was only more snow I saw, freezing
completely the fists and fingers of the fruit trees.
You had no intention to smile away your orchard.

Mother Russia's iron militia's a monster,
the thunder of Cossack horses
is a long storm you lip-read the Czar by.
Your mother knuckles the washboard into your teens,
but plans your escape. Your father sends money.
You in your orchard still fill the wooden baskets,
while the too-long-perfect bruise and fall.

Now I want you as you were before they hurt you,
irreparably as you were as in another country.
The harvest moon, sunset's clockwork, can show us
what to pick, but not whom to pick on.
Step here with me, and stay, and blame the birds
whose unschooled bedlam in the sweltering cherries
is all the blame and harm a tree can bear.

Garlic

Russian penicillin — that was the magic
of garlic, a party and cure. Sure,
you'll wrestle the flowers for fixings,
tap roots and saw branch for the ooze
of health, but you'll never get better.
I say you're living a life of leisure,
if life is life and leisure leisure.

The heart's half a prophet: it hurts
with the crabapple floating on top,
it aches just to know of the ocean —
the Old Country split off from the New —
and the acts of scissors inside you.
The heart of the East European,
poor boiler, is always born broken.

The sore heart weighs too much
for its own good. And Jewish health
is like snow in March, sometimes April.
The brothers who took their medicine
with you (garlic!) are dead now too.
The herb that beat back fever and sore
went home to its family: the lilies.

Trying to Catch Fire

You go out when the sky is dark brown,
and the air is thick lotion,
though your son says the sky is still blue
(the son's job is to say it is the same).
You go out when the best drink on earth
is water, and the sun is a lion on fire
still, but gone from your sight and mind.

The son's job is to say the future
(maybe high blue will stand over us tomorrow).
When the sky is dark brown, you go out
and turn your thoughts to the bushes and your face
to the lithe tops of trees, whereas some
are stunted and some are twisted and then some
are old and wrinkled and they are perfect.

You stand close as possible to the perfect ones,
waiting for lightning. While you wait,
you worry an old saw: that the tree is "like"
a family, its branches to high heaven
(and there, blue luster or age's browning),
its roots sucking life from the dead. That's
a thought you can follow, inside, where you do.

You Would Know

That you, Father, are "in my mind,"
some will argue, who cherish the present
but flee the past. They haven't my need
to ask, What was I? Asking instead,
What am I?, they see themselves bejeweled
and wingèd. Because they would fly and have value,
their answers are pretty but false:

the fixings of facile alchemists,
preferring their stones to brains.
The brain, remember, is not foolproof
either, and does and does until it can't.
Sodden, quivering, crossed and recrossed,
the mind can become a headstone
or be malice stuffed with fish.

Everything changes so quickly. You who were
are no longer and what I was I'm not.
Am I to know myself, except as I was?
The rest is catchy, self-promising, false.
Oh please write to me, and tell me.
I just want to be happy again. That's
what I was, happy, maybe am, you would know.

Little Father Poem

We must stay away from our fathers,
who have big ears. We must stay away
from our fathers, who are the snow.
We must avoid the touch of the leaves
who are our proud fathers. We must
watch out for Father underfoot. Father
forgave us when we did nothing wrong,
Father made us well when we were healthy,
now Father wants to support us
when we weigh nothing, Father in his grave
gives us everything we ever wanted,
in a boat crossing who-knows-where,
mist flat over the water,
the sand smooth because soft.

Temper

The seed, in its grave,
is the firmest line of labor.
A man woos havoc to undertake
the destruction of a dam in a drought.

Weren't you wound up to be metal
rulers for the hocus-pocus?
The great face of the earth
is pained to be nothing without you:

a sopping interdependence
to make bricks from mud and a family
from seed, and anger
clear through to the center.

Stars Which See, Stars Which Do Not See

1977

The Self and the Mulberry

I wanted to see the self, so I looked at the mulberry.
It had no trouble accepting its limits,
yet defining and redefining a small area
so that any shape was possible, any movement.
It stayed put, but was part of all the air.
I wanted to learn to be there and not there
like the continually changing, slightly moving
mulberry, wild cherry and particularly the willow.
Like the willow, I tried to weep without tears.
Like the cherry tree, I tried to be sturdy and productive.
Like the mulberry, I tried to keep moving.
I couldn't cry right, couldn't stay or go.
I kept losing parts of myself like a soft maple.
I fell ill like the elm. That was the end
of looking in nature to find a natural self.
Let nature think itself not manly enough!
Let nature wonder at the mystery of laughter.
Let nature hypothesize man's indifference to it.
Let nature take a turn at saying what love is!

Unable to Wake in the Heat

I can hold up my head, if barely.
Parts of the body reassemble
as in a middle movement of Brahms.
At the porch screens, large ferns
try to brush away the summer spiders.
They go on combing the muggy air
because they are strong and wide,
but the tiger lilies droop their heads
and the willow, always a leaner,
shakes her long hair in a slow dance.

There is a wonderful hallucination
in this — the consciousness of not waking,
the dimness, the weight of the body.
The head weighs the most, unbearably heavy,
and the eyes are like steel under blankets.
The head falls, finally, to the chest,
the back of the neck numb with straining,
but we know we could go even farther.
We hear music far back in our not-knowing.
Our faces relax: nothing odd there.

The Mystery of Emily Dickinson

Sometimes the weather goes on for days
but you were different. You were divine.
While the others wrote more and longer,
you wrote much more and much shorter.
I held your white dress once: 12 buttons.
In the cupola, the wasps struck glass
as hard to escape as you hit your sound
again and again asking Welcome. No one.

Except for you, it were a trifle:
This morning, not much after dawn,
in level country, not New England's,
through leftovers of summer rain I
went out ragtag to the curb, only
a sleepy householder at his routine
bending to trash, when a young girl
in a white dress your size passed,

so softly!, carrying her shoes. It must be
she surprised me — her barefoot quick-step
and the earliness of the hour, your dress —
or surely I'd have spoken of it sooner.
I should have called to her, but a neighbor
wore that look you see against happiness.
I won't say anything would have happened
unless there was time, and eternity's plenty.

Trinket

I love watching the water
ooze through the crack in the fern pot,
it's a small thing

that slows time
and steadies
and gives me ideas of becoming

having nothing to do
with ambition or even reaching,
it isn't necessary at such times

to describe this,
it's no image for mean keeping,
it's no thing that small

but presence.
Other men look at the ocean,
and I do too,

though it is too many
presences for any
to absorb.

It's this other,
a little water, used, appearing
slowly around the sounds

of oxygen and small frictions,
that gives the self
the notion of the self

one is always losing
until these tiny embodiments
small enough to contain it.

The Wild Cherry Tree Out Back

The leaves are kites.
What are their goals?

In snow and sun
it files upward — to where?

It more than fills
the painting one might have made.

It shadows and shrinks
the person who might have stood

beneath its reaching.
It seems to make its own light.

Let me be like that tree,
one might have said,

before the carving
had come far from the wood,

before the map was a shoe
and the branches were oars.

That was before
we could piss in a drawer,

when snow and sun were tact,
the tree too personal for words.

Let me be like that tree,
putting to rest

the spring
and wandering.

Two Pictures of a Leaf

If I make up this leaf
in the shape of a fan, the day's cooler
and drier than any tree. But if
under a tree I place before me
this same leaf as on a plate,
dorsal side up and then its ribs
set down like the ribs of a fish —
then I know that fish are dead to us
from the trees, and the leaf
sprawls in the net of fall to be
boned and eaten while the wind gasps.
Ah then, the grounds are a formal ruin
whereon the lucky who lived
come to resemble so much that does not.

Stars Which See, Stars Which Do Not See

They sat by the water. The fine women
had large breasts, tightly checked.
At each point, at every moment,
they seemed happy by the water.
The women wore hats like umbrellas
or carried umbrellas shaped like hats.
The men wore no hats and the water,
which wore no hats, had that well-known
mirror finish which tempts sailors.
Although the men and women seemed at rest
they were looking toward the river
and some way out into it but not beyond.
The scene was one of hearts and flowers
though this may be unfair. Nevertheless,
it was probable that the Seine had hurt them,
that they were "taken back" by its beauty
to where a slight breeze broke the mirror
and then its promise, but never the water.

To No One In Particular

Whether you sing or scream,
the process is the same.
You start, inside yourself,
a small explosion, the difference
being that in the scream
the throat is squeezed so that
the back of the tongue
can taste the brain's fear.
Also, spittle and phlegm
are components of the instrument.
I guess it would be possible
to take someone by the throat
and give him a good beating.
All the while, though, some fool
would be writing down the notes
of the victim, underscoring
this phrase, lightening this one,
adding a grace note and a trill
and instructions in one of those languages
revered for its vowels.
But all the time, it's consonants
coming from the throat.
Here's the one you were throttling,
still gagging out the guttural *ch* —
the throat-clearing, Yiddish *ch* —
and other consonants spurned by
opera singers and English teachers.
He won't bother you again.
He'll scrape home to take it out
on his wife, more bestial consonants
rising in pitch until spent.
Then he'll lock a leg over her
and snore, and all the time

he hasn't said a word we can repeat.
Even though we all speak his language.
Even though the toast in our throats
in the morning has a word for us —
not at all like bread in rain,
but something grittier in something
thicker, going through what we are.
Even though we snort and sniffle,
cough, hiccup, cry and come
and laugh until our stomachs turn.
Who will write down this language?
Who will do the work necessary?
Who will gag on a chicken bone
for observation? Who will breathe perfectly
under water? Whose slow murder
will disprove for all time
an alphabet meant to make sense?
Listen! I speak to you in one tongue,
but every moment that ever mattered to me
occurred in another language.
Starting with my first word.
To no one in particular.

Written During Depression: How to Be Happy

To be happy,
a man must love death
and failure. Then,
however great the flash
of this moment or that bit
of life's work, there
will come always another moment
to be appreciated because
fading or crumbling. If,
however, a man loves
life, there can be no end to it,
nor hope. If a man loves
reason, eventually he
will find none. If he loves
the interest of others,
he will be made to apologize
continually for his own being.
If he loves form, all
that he does or knows will
come, not to nothing, but
to that other possibility
of meaninglessness: everything.
That is why "the shape of things
to come" is a phrase littered with
tracks into the bush
where the pure primitive
is a headhunter's delusion,
and why, my dear, I love you.

"Gradually, It Occurs to Us..."

Gradually, it occurs to us
that none of it was necessary —
not the heavy proclaiming
the sweat and length of our love
when, together, we thought it the end;
nor the care we gave your dress,
smoothing it as we would the sky;
nor the inevitable envelope of This-
is-the-time-we-always-knew-would-come,
and good-bye. All that was ever needed
was all that we had to offer,
and we have had it all. I have your absence.
And have left myself inside you.
Now when you come back to me,
or I to you, don't give it a thought.
This time, when first we fall into bed,
we won't know who we are, or where,
or what is going to happen to us.
Time is memory. We have the time.

What Is There

When the grass, wet and matted,
is thick as a dry lawn is not,
I think of a kind of printing —
a page at a time, and the thick
paper hung up to dry, its
deep impressions filled and shapely
where ink is held and hardens.

And I wonder then at the underside
of those damp sheets of grass —
the muddy blood of those buried
coming up into the flattened green
as I press it underfoot, and pass,
and the sun drawing moisture
until we accept what is written there.

Dew at the Edge of a Leaf

The broader leaves collect
enough to see early
by a wide spread of moonlight,
and they shine!, shine! —
who are used to turning
faces to the light.

Looking up is farthest.
From here or under any tree,
I know what will transpire:
leaves in their watery halos have
an overhead-to-underfoot career,
and thrive toward falling.

In a passage of time and water,
I am halfway — a leaf in July?
In August? I take no pity.
Everything green is turning brown,
it's true, but then too
everything turning brown is green!

By Different Paths

We have all had our heads in a book
on the trouble with love
or, say, by a river looking for answers
downstream we have come to a place
somewhere inside us as smooth as
the guarded heart of an acorn
and how we came to be lost so
completely to one feeling
no one can say.

Ah, rules: of trees toward light
and water, cork and dead men to the surface,
some would say lunatics to the fringes.
But you and I, by different paths,
have arrived upstream from many possible
replies — I hope a craggy surface
won't prevent you — and the deaths we drop
stay down, light-headedness also.
Now love is easy, pleases; no answer.

An Introduction to My Anthology

Such a book must contain —
it always does! — a disclaimer.
I make no such. For here
I have collected all the best —
the lily from the field among them,
forget-me-nots and mint weed,
a rose for whoever expected it,
and a buttercup for the children
to make their noses yellow.

Here is clover for the lucky
to roll in, and milkweed to clatter,
a daisy for one judgment,
and a violet for when he loves you
or if he loves you not and why not.
Those who sniff and say no,
These are the wrong ones (and
there always are such people!) —
let them go elsewhere, and quickly!

For you and I, who have made it this far,
are made happy by occasions
requiring orchids, or queenly arrangements
and even a bird-of-paradise,
but happier still by the flowers of
circumstance, cattails of our youth,
field grass and bulrush. I have included
the devil's paintbrush
but only as a peacock among barn fowl.

Watching the Bomber Pass Over

How can we speak of eyes and seasons
(or a tree-sore in the shape of a horse-collar)
when the eyes are yanked upward
and the lightest season made thicker
by the indifference of its metal?
And that is not everything, for in
the time it takes to start a wind,
this romance of progress, this story
of wings, this monstrous dare,
can be brought crushingly to earth.

How can we bend to the nibbled bark
of the sapling, and fence round
the wind-torn and weeping bushes,
when the moon which was our candy father
is a stone's throw and a dry station?
How stake tomatoes and thin the lettuce
when war is a question of permission,
and the history of the human passion
is written by a clock seeking a promotion,
and History loves Hitler, not Schweitzer?

You know the way the water for flowers
passes them by and remains a while below
and then is slowly drawn upward
lighter for the settling, leaving its grit,
without which it would never have fallen,
to the soil: well, that is the way it is.
Grief falls everywhere. How joyful we are!
Around us spring up lives like ours,
not one of us has all the cares of the world!,
not one of us escapes some little happiness!

To Dorothy

You are not beautiful, exactly.
You are beautiful, inexactly.
You let a weed grow by the mulberry
and a mulberry grow by the house.
So close, in the personal quiet
of a windy night, it brushes the wall
and sweeps away the day till we sleep.

A child said it, and it seemed true:
"Things that are lost are all equal."
But it isn't true. If I lost you,
the air wouldn't move, nor the tree grow.
Someone would pull the weed, my flower.
The quiet wouldn't be yours. If I lost you,
I'd have to ask the grass to let me sleep.

Gemwood

to Nathan and Jason, our sons

In the *shoppes*
they're showing "gemwood":
the buffed-up flakes of dye-fed pines —
bright concentrics or bull's-eyes,
wide-eyed on the rack of
this newest "joint effort
of man and nature." But then

those life-lines circling
each target chip of "gemwood"
look less like eyes, yours or mine,
when we have watched a while.
They are more like the whorls
at the tips of our fingers,
which no one can copy. Even on

the photocopy Jason made of
his upraised hands, palms down
to the machine, they do not appear.
His hands at five years old —
why did we want to copy them, and
why does the gray yet clear print
make me sad? That summer,

the Mad River followed us
through Vermont — a lusher state than
our own. A thunderous matinee
of late snows, and then the peak
at Camels Hump was bleached.
As a yellow pear is to the sky —
that was our feeling. We had with us

a rat from the lab — no, a pet
we'd named, a pure friend who changed
our minds. When it rained near
the whole of the summer, in that
cabin Nathan made her a social creature.
She was all our diversion, and brave.
That's why, when she died

in the heat of our car
one accidental day we didn't intend,
it hurt her master first and most,
being his first loss like that,
and the rest of our family felt bad
even to tears, for a heart that small.
We buried her by the road

in the Adirondack Mountains,
and kept our way to Iowa.
Now it seems to me the heart
must enlarge to hold the losses
we have ahead of us. I hold to
a certain sadness the way others
search for joy, though I like joy.

Home, sunlight cleared the air
and all the green's of consequence. Still
when it ends, we won't remember
that it ended. If parents must receive
the sobbing, that is nothing
when put next to the last crucial fact
of who is doing the crying.

These Green-Going-to-Yellow

1981

He Said To

crawl *toward* the machine guns
except to freeze
for explosions and flares.
It was still ninety degrees
at night in North Carolina,
August, rain and all.
The tracer bullets wanted
our asses, which we swore to keep
down, and the highlight
of this preposterous exercise
was finding myself in mud
and water during flares. I
hurried in the darkness —
over things and under things —
to reach the next black pool
in time, and once
I lay in the cool salve that
so suited all I had become
for two light-ups of the sky.
I took one inside and one
face of two watches I ruined
doing things like that,
and made a watch that works.
From the combat
infiltration course and
common sense, I made a man
to survive the Army, which means
that I made a man to survive
being a man.

We Had Seen a Pig

I

One man held the huge pig down
and the other stuck an ice pick
into the jugular, which is when
we started to pay attention.
The blood rose ten feet with force
while the sow swam on its back
as if to cut its own neck.
Its fatty back smacked the slippery
cement while the assassins shuffled
to keep their balance, and the bloody
fountain rose and fell back and rose
less and less high, until
the red plume reentered the pig
at the neck, and the belly collapsed
and the pig face went dull.

2

I knew the pig
was the butcher's, whose game
lived mainly behind our garage.
Sometimes turkeys, always
roosters and sheep. Once the windmill
turned two days without stopping.
The butcher would walk in his apron
straight for the victim. The others
would scratch and babble
and get in the way.
Then the butcher would lead the animal
to the back door of his shop,
stopping to kill it on a stump.
It was always evening, after closing.

The sea breeze would be rising,
cloaking the hour in brine.

3

The pig we saw slaughtered
was more than twice anything
shut up in the patch
we trespassed to make havoc.
Since the butcher was Italian,
not Jewish, that would be his pig.
Like the barber who carried
a cigar box of bets
to the stationery store, like
the Greek who made sweets
and hid Greek illegals,
immigrant "submarines,"
the butcher had a business, his
business, by which he took
from our hands the cleaver and serrated
knife for the guts,
and gave us back in butcher paper
and outer layers of brown wrapping
our lives for their cries.

4

Hung up to drain, the great pig,
hacked into portions,
looked like a puzzle
we could put together in the freezer
to make a picture of
a pig of course, a map, clothes or other things
when we looked.

The Canal at Rye

Don't let them tell you —
the women or the men —
they knew me.
You knew me.
Don't let them tell you
I didn't love your mother.
I loved her.
Or let them tell you.
Do you remember Rye? —
where the small fishing boats,
deprived of the receding sea,
took the tide out,
a canal so thin they had to go
single file, sails of suns,
while the red sun rose.
That town was old.
A great novelist lived there.
Do you know him?
Not many will be reading
his long sentences.
And they are punished.
For that is *our* sentence: to be
dumb in a passage we think turns
from darkness to light
but doesn't. Turn back
to art, including the sentence.
It is also the world. Whoever understands
the sentence understands
his or her life. There are reasons
not to, reasons too
to believe or not to. But
reasons do not complete an argument.
The natural end and extension

of language
is nonsense. Yet there is safety
only there. That is why Mr. Henry James
wrote that way —
out with the tide, but farther.

The Last Thing I Say

to a thirteen-year-old sleeping,
tone of an angel, breath of a soft wing,
I say through an upright dark space
as I narrow it pulling the door
sleepily to let the words go surely into
the bedroom until I close them in
for good, a night watchman's–worth
of grace and a promise for morning
not so far from some God's first notion
that the world be an image by first light
so much better than pictures of hope
drawn by firelight in ashes,
so much clearer, too, a young person
wanting to be a man might draw one finger
along an edge of this world and it
would slice a mouth there
to speak blood and then should he put that wound
into the mouth of his face,
he will be kissed there and taste
the salt of his father as he lowers
himself from his son's high bedroom
in the heaven of his image of
a small part of himself and sweet dreams.

To an Adolescent Weeping Willow

I don't know what you think you're doing,
sweeping the ground. You
do it so easily, backhanded, forehanded.
You hardly bend. Really, you sway.
What can it mean
when a thing is so easy?

I threw dirt on my father's floor.
Not dirt, but a chopped green
dirt which picked up dirt.

I pushed the push broom.
I oiled the wooden floor of the store.

He bent over and lifted the coal
into the coal stove. With the back of the shovel
he came down on the rat just topping the bin
and into the fire.

What do you think? — Did he sway?
Did he kiss a rock for luck?
Did he soak up water
and climb into light and turn and turn?

Did he weep and weep in the yard?

Yes, I think he did. Yes,
now I think he did.

So Willow, you come sweep my floor.
I have no store.
I have a yard. A big yard.

I have a song to weep.
I have a cry.

You who rose up from the dirt,
because I put you there
and like to walk my head in under
your earliest feathery branches —
what can it mean
when a thing is so easy?

It means you are a boy.

These Green-Going-to-Yellow

This year,
I'm raising the emotional ante,
putting my face
in the leaves to be stepped on,
seeing myself among them, that is;
that is, likening
leaf-vein to artery, leaf to flesh,
the passage of a leaf in autumn
to the passage of autumn,
branch-tip and winter spaces
to possibilities, and possibility
to God. Even on East 61st Street
in the blowzy city of New York,
someone has planted a gingko
because it has leaves like fans like hands,
hand-leaves, and sex. Those lovely
Chinese hands on the sidewalks
so far from delicacy
or even, perhaps, another gender of gingko —
do we see them?
No one ever treated us so gently
as these green-going-to-yellow hands
fanned out where we walk.
No one ever fell down so quietly
and lay where we would look
when we were tired or embarrassed,
or so bowed down by humanity
that we had to watch out lest our shoes stumble,
and looked down not to look up
until something looked like parts of people
where we were walking. We have no
experience to make us see the gingko
or any other tree,

and, in our admiration for whatever grows tall
and outlives us,
we look away, or look at the middles of things,
which would not be our way
if we truly thought we were gods.

A Motor

The heavy, wet, guttural
small-plane engine
fights for air, and goes down in humid darkness
about where the airport should be.
I take a lot for granted,
not pleased to be living under the phlegm-
soaked, gaseous, foggy and irradiated
heavens whose angels wear collars in propjets
and live elsewhere in Clean Zones,
but figuring the air is full of sorrows.

I don't blame
the quick use of the entire earth
on the boozy
pilot
come down to get a dose of cobalt
for his cancer. He's got
a little life left, if
he doesn't have to take all day to reach it.
With the black patches
inside him, and
the scars and the streaks and the sick stomach,

his life is more and more like
that of the lowliest child chimney sweep
in the mind of the great insensible,
William Blake. William Blake,
the repeated one, Blake, half mad,
half remembered,
who knew his anatomy, down to
the little-observed muscle in the shoulder
that lifts the wing.

The little London chimney sweeper
reaches up and reaches down.
In his back,
every vertebra is separated from the long
hours of stretching.
With one deep, tired breath,
the lungs go black.

By the Holiday Company crane,
adding a level to the hospital,
on the highest land in the county,
heavy sits the pure-white Air Care
helicopter, with
its bulging eye.
It has kept many going, a good buy,
something.

Now someone I know says Blake
in anger,
angry for his brother in the factory
and his sister on the ward,
but tonight I have no more anger
than the muscle
that lifts my knee when I walk.

Another pleads with the ocean
that the words for
suffering and trouble
take place in a sound that will be all sounds
and in the tidal roll
of all our lives and every event,
but I am silent by water,

and am less to such power
than a failed lung.

And I think it is only a clever trick to know
that one thing may be contained
in another. Hence,
Blake in the sweep, one in the ground
in one in the air,
myself in the clinic for runaway cells,
now and later.

Drawn by Stones, by Earth, by Things That Have Been in the Fire

1984

White Clover

Once when the moon was out about three-quarters
and the fireflies who are the stars
of backyards
were out about three-quarters
and about three-fourths of all the lights
in the neighborhood
were on because people can be at home,
I took a not so innocent walk
out among the lawns,
navigating by the light of lights,
and there there were many hundreds of moons
on the lawns
where before there was only polite grass.
These were moons on long stems,
their long stems giving their greenness
to the center of each flower
and the light giving its whiteness to the tops
of the petals. I could say
it was light from stars
touched the tops of flowers and no doubt
something heavenly reaches what grows outdoors
and the heads of men who go hatless,
but I like to think we have a world
right here, and a life
that isn't death. So I don't say it's better
to be right here. I say this is where
many hundreds of core-green moons
gigantic to my eye
rose because men and women had sown green grass,
and flowered to my eye in man-made light,
and to some would be as fire in the body
and to others a light in the mind
over all their property.

Unless It Was Courage

Again today, balloons aloft in the hazy *here*,
three heated, airy, basket-toting balloons,
three triangular boasts ahead against the haze
of summer and the gravity of onrushing fall —
these win me from the wavery *chrr*-ing of locusts
that fills these days the air between the trees,
from the three trembly outspreading cocoons hanging
on an oak so old it might have been weighed down
by the very thought of hundreds of new butterflies,
and from all other things that come in threes
or seem to be arranged. These *are* arranged,
they are the perfection of mathematics as idea,
they have lifted off by making the air greater —
nothing else was needed unless it was courage —
and today they do not even drag a shadow.

It was only a week ago I ran beneath one.
All month overhead had passed the jetliners,
the decorated company planes, the prop jobs
and great crows of greed and damage (I saw one
dangle a white snake from its bill as it flew),
and all month I had looked up from everywhere
to see what must seem from other galaxies
the flies of heaven. Then quickly my chance came,
and I ran foolish on the grass with my neck bent
to see straight up into the great resonant cavity
of one grandly wafting, rising, bulbous, whole
balloon, just to see nothing for myself. That
was enough, it seemed, as it ran skyward and away.
There I was, unable to say what I'd seen.
But I was happy, and my happiness made others happy.

Jane Was With Me

Jane was with me
the day the rain dropped a squirrel *like that.*
An upside-down embrace,
a conical explosion from the sky,
a thick flowering of sudden water —
whatever it was,
the way it happened is
that first the trees grew a little,
and then they played music
and breathed songs and applauded themselves,
and that made the squirrel
surrender to nothing but the beauty
of a wet tree
about to shake its upper body like the devil.
And of course, of course,
he went out on that tree just as far as he could
when things were not so beautiful
and that was it: hard onto the roof of our car
before he could set his toes.

The flat whack of the body.
He lay in the street breathing and bleeding
until I could get back,
and then he looked me in the eye exactly.
Pasted to the concrete by his guts,
he couldn't lift, or leave, or live.
And so I brought the car and put its right tire
across his head. If in between
the life part and the death part,
there is another part,
a time of near-death,
we have come to know its length and its look
exactly — in this life always near death.

But there's something else.
Jane was with me.
After the rain, the trees were prettier yet.
And if I were a small animal with a wide tail,
I would trust them too. Especially
if Jane were with me.

Drawn by Stones, by Earth, by Things That Have Been in the Fire

I can tell you about this because I have held in my hand
the little potter's sponge called an "elephant ear."
Naturally, it's only a tiny version of an ear,
but it's the thing you want to pick up out of the toolbox
when you wander into the deserted ceramics shop
down the street from the cave where the fortune-teller works.
Drawn by stones, by earth, by things that have been in the fire.

The elephant ear listens to the side of the vase
as it is pulled upward from a dome of muddy clay.
The ear listens to the outside wall of the pot
and the hand listens to the inside wall of the pot,
and between them a city rises out of dirt and water.
Inside this city live the remains of animals,
animals who prepared for two hundred years to be clay.

Rodents make clay, and men wearing spectacles make clay,
though the papers they were signing go up in flames
and nothing more is known of these long documents
except by those angels who divine in our ashes.
Kings and queens of the jungle make clay
and royalty and politicians make clay although
their innocence stays with their clothes until unraveled.

There is a lost soldier in every ceramic bowl.
The face on the dinner plate breaks when the dish does
and lies for centuries unassembled in the soil.
These things that have the right substance to begin with,
put into the fire at temperatures that melt glass,
keep their fingerprints forever, it is said,
like inky sponges that walk away in the deep water.

Starfish

His entire body is but one hand, severed at the wrist. It lies on the sand in the late afternoon as if sunning itself. As he dries, he reaches ever more arthritically for the light itself with which to brown his palm. In this regard, his futility is unsurpassed.

You may pick him up now. Dead hand in your live hand. The mound of flesh just behind the thumb has been planed down and the soft tissue, tissue that will never tan, seems to have endured much scraping and dragging on the roughest edges of the sea, and to have fought back by raising its hackles, as it were, until it has become a hand of tiny spikes, but spikes nonetheless. Rub him in your palm, if you like. His hand is tougher than your own.

Of course, this starfish that we know is only the version run aground, becalmed, out of its element, preserved, petrified. In its lifetime, which we have missed entirely, it was soft, it was spongy, it was bread to the sea. Then, it molded itself to its element, water, not as a hand closes around a prized possession to become a fist, but as a wheel becomes motion without losing its shape even for a moment.

The starfish, alive, was a kind of wheel. The sea was its air, as all around us in what we call a universe are stars in space like fish in the ocean. Like fish, we know them only at a distance, we approach closer to them by means of glass and mirrors, we grow silent in the presence of the mysterious nature of them, we may only imagine touching them when they have been cast up on the beach or thrown down from light.

Such is our conception of heaven, from which it seems we are forever finding souvenirs, signals, clues. We have no way of knowing whether, at any single moment, we are being led toward a heaven that follows upon our lives or toward one that precedes it, or indeed whether or not these may be the same. Is it not then natural that we look down in the light and up in the darkness, and is it not also ironic that it requires a dark, absorbent object to stop our gaze in the former while it takes a moment of hard light to focus us in the latter? We shall never know the end of our thoughts, nor where they began.

Return to our starfish now. Time has given it a new, earthy odor.

Felt but Not Touched

Seattle

That light behind the Olympics at supper hour —
it takes a sky of clouds from here to there
to spot the sun, seam and snow just right.
That pulsating light, a sizable incandescence
out of the grayness — that's the wing or tail of a plane.
The roundness of things — that's knowledge, a new way
to touch it here. (On the plains, we see Earth curve,
and I have seen the sun melt into the ocean elsewhere
and then call a color or two it left behind down.)

Then it is dark. The great streak of sunlight
that showed our side of snowy peaks has gone ahead.
Those bumps on the holly tree we passed
getting home for the late afternoon view from upstairs —
next to them, some smaller trees and a porch,
and next to that the streaky windows and then
the whole household getting ready to make the break
into spring — and sometimes in late winter we can't
sit still for connecting time at both ends.

If anything we do or don't will keep the world
for others, it will need such distant knowledge — beyond
experience, provable by ones, felt but not touched.
And as we watch the light in the distance move on and around,
and the air at mountain height take up the cause of snow,
all that is beneath us that is not light has stopped.

Trees As Standing for Something

1

More and more it seems I am happy with trees
and the light touch of exhausted morning.
I wake happy with her soft breath on my neck.
I wake happy but I am happier yet.
For my loves are like the leaves in summer.
But oh!, when they fall, and I wake with a start,
will I feel the sting of betrayal and ask, What is this
love, if it has to end, even in death,
or if one might lose it even during a life?
Who will care for such a thing?
Better to cut it down where it stands.
Better to burn it, and to burn with it,
than to turn around to see one's favorite gone.

2

It began when they cut down the elm and I let them.
When the corkscrew willow withered and I said nothing.
Then when the soft maple began to blow apart,
when the apple tree succumbed to poison,
the pine to a matrix of bugs, the oak to age,
it was my own limbs that were torn off, or so it seemed,
and my love, which had lived through many storms,
died, again and again. Again and again, it perished.
What was I to say then but Oh, Oh, Oh, Oh, Oh!
Now you see a man at peace, happy and happier yet,
with her breath on the back of his neck in the morning,
and of course you assume it must always have been this way.
But what was I to say, then and now, but Oh! and Oh! Oh!

Instructions to Be Left Behind

I've included this letter in the group
to be put into the cigar box — the one
with the rubber band around it you will find
sometime later. I thought you might
like to have an example of the way in which
some writing works. I may not say anything
very important or phrase things just-so,
but I think you will pay attention anyway
because it matters to you — I'm sure it does,
no one was ever more loved than I was.

What I'm saying is, your deep attention
made things matter — made art,
made science and business
raised to the power of goodness, and sport
likewise raised a level beyond.
I am not attaching to this a photograph
though no doubt you have in your mind's eye
a clear image of me in several expressions
and at several ages all at once — which is
the great work of imagery beyond the merely
illustrative. Should I stop here for a moment?

These markings, transliterations though they are
from prints of fingers, and they from heart
and throat and corridors the mind guards,
are making up again in you the one me
that otherwise would not survive that manyness
daisies proclaim and the rain sings much of.
Because I love you, I can almost imagine
the eye for detail with which you remember
my face in places indoors and out and far-flung,
and you have only to look upward to see

in the plainest cloud the clearest lines
and in the flattest field your green instructions.

Shall I rest a moment in green instructions?
Writing is all and everything, when you care.
The kind of writing that grabs your lapels
and shakes you — that's for when you don't care
or even pay attention. This isn't that kind.
While you are paying your close kind of attention,
I might be writing the sort of thing you think
will last — as it is happening, now, for you.
While I was here to want this, I wanted it,
and now that I am your wanting me to be myself
again, I think myself right up into being
all that you (and I too) wanted to be: You.

The Nest

The day the birds were lifted from my shoulders,
the whole sky was blue, a long-imagined effect
had taken hold, and a small passenger plane
was beating the earth with its wings
as it swung over the bean fields toward home.
A fat car barely traveled a narrow road
while I waited at the bottom of a hill.
People around me were speaking loudly
but I heard only whispers, and stepped away.

You understand, I was given no choice.
For a long time, I was tired of whatever it was
that dug its way into my shoulders for balance
and whispered in my ears, and hung on for dear life
among tall narrow spaces in the woods
and in thickets and crowds, like those of success,
with whom one mingles at parties and in lecture halls.
In the beginning, there was this or that...
but always on my shoulders that which had landed.

That was life, and it went on in galleries
and shopping plazas, in museums and civic centers,
much like the life of any responsible man
schooled in the marriage of history and culture
and left to learn the rest at the legs of women.
In furtive rooms, in passing moments, the sea
reopened a door at its depth, trees spoke
from the wooden sides of houses, bodies became
again the nests in the naked tree.

After that, I was another person,
without knowing why or how, and after that,
I lived naked in a new world where the sun

broke through windows to grasp entire families
and crept between trees to wash down streets
without disturbing any object, in a world
where a solitary kiss blew down a door.
The day the birds were lifted from my shoulders,
it killed me — and almost cost me a life...

The Facts of Life

This pebble never thought it would surface here
where I came walking to scuff it, wreck it, bother it,
and utterly transform it from a simple creature
of limited experience in the darkness of its mother
into a highly valued, polished star of daylight.
I, of course, was just passing the time by rolling it
back and forth under the sole of my shoe.

A psychiatrist would say I was worried at the time,
but I would say I was worried *all* of the time —
here with the trees taking sick and even the healthiest
rocking in the dirt from this disaster and that one,
so that bare plots of land where prairie grass shone
took up with tumult and history, forever locked,
and rocks appeared on cleared land without warning.

It's as if something in nature were asking my help,
but modestly, reluctantly, as politely as a black shoe.
I stood where I might see what was asked for,
by the dry sites of immense basements for new buildings
where pipe was being laid in the dusty man-made rivers
which run down everywhere beneath the deepest roots.
I stood and worked my foot back and forth like a rolling pin.

Out of the throat of the world, a pebble emerged.
And it said nothing, or was muffled before it could speak
by the innocence of bystanders, by the facts of life.
Dingy and shipwrecked, the buildings rose higher.
When the men broke from work under the threat of rain,
I took that star of daylight, my little marble,
into my hand, where it helped me to cut my way home.

Days of Time

Gone into the woods, they'll say, only because
I preferred the company of trees, any kind of tree,
to the company of... It was a day like this one,
in the dark season, a time when one sits in the center
avoiding the flat wind that blows through the walls,
that time when icy vapors hover above the river
and the big pines move like old men in dark clothes
for an important occasion: the days of time, time of time.

Gone into the sea, they'll say, just because
I loved to walk on the darkened sand at the weed line
near to the scalloped edge of the ocean, and there
felt on the soles of my feet as the spent waves receded
the termites of ocean floors and the crab imprint
that gives the galaxy a picture of the galaxy.
It was a wide day in the sunshine, but narrow in the shadows,
when I walked around a bend in the beach and stayed.

Disappeared into thin air, they'll say, because
I stopped to look up at a giant red fan in the clouds
and a picture of four bakers peeking over the horizon,
and counted the wooden thread-spools in a cigar box.
It was a day like this one: sulphur hung in the air,
somewhere the earth vented the steam at its core.
It was a day in the future, just like this in the future,
when the melting wax no longer seemed to betray the candle.

One of the Animals

Why does a dog get sick?
— You tell me.

What does he do about it?
— You tell me.

Does it make a difference?
— You tell me.

Does he live or die?
— You tell me.

Does it make a difference?
— That one I know.

Does it prepare you?
— That one I know too.

Will we know what to do?
— You tell me.

The Stones

One night in my room
many stones brought together over the years,
each bearing the gouges and pinpricks
of sea and shore life,
and each weighted according to the sea
which first chisels a slate
and then washes it and later writes on it
with an eraser —
these stones, large and small, flat,
rounded, conical, shapely or rough-hewn,
discussed their origins,
and then got around to me. One of them,
the white one full of holes
that wipes off on your hands, said
that he thinks I carry much sadness,
the weight of a heart full of stones,
and that I bring back these others
so that I might live among the obvious
heaviness of the world.
But another said that I carried him
six months in Spain
in a pants pocket and lifted him out
each night to place on the dresser,
and although he is small and flat,
like a planet seen from the moon,
I often held him up to the light,
and this is because I am able to lift
the earth itself. And isn't this
happiness? But a third stone spoke
from where it stood atop papers
and accused me of trying to manage
the entire world, which for the most part
is neither myself nor not myself,

but is also the air around the rim
of a moving wheel, the space beyond Space,
the water within water,
and the weight within the stone.
Then they all asked what right had I
to be happy or unhappy,
when the language of stones
was no different
from the language of a white lump of dung
among the excellent vegetables.

Personal Reasons

Your hair — short, long; stars, a bed
under stars, moon; your stars, your moon,
your embrace, your circumstances, my
buttons, your earrings; your collections
of moonlight in darkened rooms — let it all
fall when it will: so surrounded are we
already by all that we have lost
to each other, we could be god and goddess,
we could be grass and sky, flower and tree,
two of anything in romantic proximity. But
we are — that's it — one man and one woman,
alike we choose to believe. But it
(you and me) wasn't always that way,
or not so very much that very way — us.

New and Selected Poems

1987

Wednesday

Gray rainwater lay on the grass in the late afternoon.
The carp lay on the bottom, resting, while dusk took shape
in the form of the first stirrings of his hunger,
and the trees, shorter and heavier, breathed heavily upward.
Into this sodden, nourishing afternoon I emerged,
partway toward a paycheck, halfway toward the weekend,
carrying the last mail and holding above still puddles
the books of noble ideas. Through the fervent branches,
carried by momentary breezes of local origin,
the palpable Sublime flickered as motes on broad leaves,
while the Higher Good and the Greater Good contended
as sap on the bark of the maples, and even I
was enabled to witness the truly Existential where it loitered
famously in the shadows as if waiting for the moon.
All this I saw in the late afternoon in the company of no one.

And of course I went back to work the next morning. Like you,
like anyone, like the rumored angels of high office,
like the demon foremen, the bedeviled janitors, like you,
I returned to my job — but now there was a match-head in
        my thoughts.
In its light, the morning increasingly flamed through the window
and, lit by nothing but mind-light, I saw that the horizon
was an idea of the eye, gilded from within, and the sun
the fiery consolation of our nighttimes, coming far.
Within this expectant air, which had waited the night indoors,
carried by — who knows? — the rhythmic jarring of brain tissue
by footsteps, by colors visible to closed eyes, by a music
in my head, knowledge gathered that could not last the day,
love and error were shaken as if by the eye of a storm,
and it would not be until quitting that such a man
might drop his arms, that he had held up all day since the dew.

Long Island

The things I did, I did because of trees,
wildflowers and weeds, because of ocean and sand,
because the dunes move about under houses built on stilts,
and the wet fish slip between your hands back into the sea,
because during the War we heard strafing across the Bay
and after the War we found shell casings with our feet.
Because old tires ringed the boat docks,
and sandbags hung from the prows of speedboats,
and every road in every country ends at the water,
and because a child thinks each room in his house big,
and if the truth be admitted, his first art galleries
were the wallpaper in his bedroom and the car lights
warming the night air as he lay in bed counting.

The things I did, I counted in wattage and ohms,
in the twelve zones that go from pure black to pure white,
in the length of the trumpet and the curves of the cornet,
in the cup of the mouthpiece. In the compass and protractor,
in the perfect beveled ruler, in abstract geometry,
and if the truth be known, in the bowing of cattails
he first read his Heracleitus and in the stretching box turtle
he found his theory of relativity and the gist of knowledge.
He did what he did. The action of his knee in walking
was not different from the over-stretching of an ocean wave,
and the proofs of triangles, cones and parallelograms
were neither more nor less than the beauty of a fast horse
which runs through the numbers of the stopwatch and past
            the finish.

The things I counted, I counted beyond the finish,
beyond rolling tar roadways that squared the fields,
where I spun on the ice, wavered in fog, sped up or idled,
and, like Perry, like Marco Polo, a young man I saw

alone walk unlit paths, encircled by rushes
and angry dogs, to the indentations of his island.
And if the truth be told, he learned of Columbus,
of Einstein, of Michelangelo, on such low roads and local waters.
Weakfish hauled weakening from the waters at night,
and the crab rowing into the light, told him in their way
that the earth moved around the sun in the same way,
with the branched mud-print of a duck's foot to read,
and life in the upturned bellies of the fishkill in the creek.

Replica

The fake Parthenon in Nashville, Stonehenge reduced by a quarter
near Maryhill on the Columbia, the little Statue of Liberty
taken from the lawn of the high school and not recovered
        for months,
Simon Rodia's Watts Towers in the tile maker's shape of a ship
to sail home in, the house in the shape of a ship near Milwaukee
where once before the river below rose up to swallow the bank,
World's Fairs where one can enter the cell of a human body
or see Paris, London, Marrakech and the Taj Mahal in
        one afternoon,
the headache that may be sinus or bad eyes or allergy or a tumor,
the bruise that was blue now yellow the effect of labor or abuse,
the cataclysmic event in a personal life not totally forgotten,
the memory of doing well that turned to unexpressed anger
just because love was everywhere preventing helpless mistakes —
achievement and perfection for the first time considered in error,
the end of life being life itself, life itself ignorance,
we never tire of making the world smaller, looking in doll houses,
and a mailman who has picked up every bright piece of glass and tile
in forty years of rounds retired to build a house of glass and tile
which is his life, no kick coming, while in a suburb of Chicago
a leaning tower of Pisa drawn to scale signals a shopping plaza
where goods come in from around the world, for the people who
        live there.
And Vico says gods and goddesses are the self writ large —
selves to make earthquakes, tornadoes, eclipses, selves to lift the sun —
and Vico says all things having been named for the namers, us,
we give a chair arms, legs, a seat and a back, a cup has its lip
and a bottle its neck, and ever after rivers flow from their headwaters
and a well-oiled engine purrs at the center of good feeling.
So take your misery down a notch in aches and pains and
        little diseases,

in years of photo albums, in journals of dreams interrupted
          by mornings,
in furniture you built yourself, in copies and imitations,
in scale-model wars and families and the age of fancy automobiles.
And when once in your life you make the big trip to the original,
chances are you'll mainly see your own face in the glass that protects
everything of which there's one only in the form of its only maker.

The Politics of an Object

The banana is stronger than the human head in the following ways: those fine threads that wave from the top knot are harder to break than hair. Should you pick one up, you cannot resist peeling it: it will have done to it what it was born to have done to it. As for endurance and sacrifice: while thousands of well-muscled laborers did not survive the cheap labor of imperialism in their republics, and others died with their mouths stuffed full of money, the banana hung on, gathering potassium. It knew the future, it knew its history, it was prepared for bruises. I have gathered the small colorful stickers applied one to a bunch until now they cover the wooden arms of the chair where I often linger in the kitchen to chat with my wife. The bananas don't last long, eaten or not. But each of the tiny stickers, each company logo, stays in place incorruptibly, and, though I am but one man, without a plan, I am keeping their names in mind. So you see? A banana is superior to a human head because it gives up without a fight. And still there is a future.

Classified

I am no more stupid now than I ever was; I am the same.
The end of tomorrow is no farther away than it ever was.
If no one had occasionally moved them, or fueled them,
the end of our todays would be frozen like a field of old bolts
in their military silos, and wouldn't that be a kick
in the flowers for all the earthshaking dreams that caught us.
Wanted: a few good men and women who won't do their jobs.

The Pill

The pill, in the pill bottle, humming like a wheel at rest, confident that the time must come when it will control the future and distance unravel to the end of time — this small round package of power, this force for lingering life or lingering death, this salt for the soul, this spice with roots in antiquity — this coated equation smaller than a fingertip embodies and contains you. And who gave it that right, who harnessed chemistry and put *things* in charge? We demand to know. We intend to hold them responsible: death would be too good for them. The search begins in the home, it begins just behind the mirror: there, in the bathroom cabinet, are the innocuous masters of our lives — the toothpaste, the deodorant, the shampoo. Someone has decreed that we should not remain during the days those briny, glistening starfish as which we crawled the bottoms of seas to suck up the smallest, reddest forms of life. It is not so bad to be in the air now, routine to live as two beings: one in the light, the other just beneath the light-tight skin of sleep. But to be the third thing: the creature that was given, by mistake, the demented brain, and now must absorb with flaccidity the daily dose of electricity that will prolong its self-knowledge. For it is one thing to be alive — the grass is alive, the pea and the potato grow, and microscopic algae stain with their living bodies the snow of the coldest regions — and another thing to *know* that one is alive. Where in philosophy was it decided that, if it is good to be able to choose, it is twice good to realize it? The argument that once raged inside the spiral corridors of a nautilus, at a depth a human being could only imagine, sings all around us like wind in the alleys, like city water in the sewers. We have not been shocked enough yet. We are not yet ready. Great areas of our brains still lie dormant like the liquid-carved underside of a coral reef. The debate rages in words and gestures. Sparks open up new hallways between logic and instinct. But it is in the dormant regions of the brain, the resonant cavities of absolute not-knowing, that life is closest to the source of life. A whole brain like that is like a head carried in on a plate. For a moment, it is one thing that looks like another thing. For a moment, everyone in the room could have sworn that it could see them, and that it blinked.

In My Nature: 3 Corrective Dialogues

To a Tree

Pine with little pines, with many arms,
with hair to sift the sunlight, with feet that grip
widely and deep, with a trunk for a spine —
you're my neighbor now, here at the window, bursting
to testify: *you can make it through the winter
in your heart. I did.* And it did, and does.

My heart was cold and hard like yours. Mine was
hidden in a fist, in a knot, like yours, mine
was mine alone. The world was snow, was covered —
if anything beat below the surface, I could not feel
it — me, the rock, the potato brought to term, me,
to whom all things were done while I stayed in this place.

I'm the kind who couldn't pick up the axe except
to lean it against the shed. I leaned it against the wind.
I shouldered it. Even after I let it fall,
I shouldered it. Today, with my blood running
and your sap running, and the world counting its shovels,
I wake to the rhythm of your Medusa load of axe handles.

The Tree Replies

To be a man is to be a sentimentalist, soft inside.
You don't stand but already you imagine a horizon
past the horizon, a purer arc of earth, a heaven —
and a pulsing under all: under snow, under soil.
Unhappy and remote, walking your eyes up a mountain
in steps, gauging the time available to you, alas,

yelling and straining, patronized by the stars,
radical, soft-living, harvested by any boss,
you swallow hard whenever you feel sleep approaching.

I'm going to give you another chance. Be like me.
Or, if it's late in your life, and you wish to be
remembered as noble, be like the axe in the air.

You can get a lot of comfort from standing up to
what doesn't move. And standing down, too — *there's*
the hard-won secret of dark places where the eyes
widen: at the bottom of the well, where the roots are,
among feelers inching toward the last drops of water.
Be willing to live like me. Be willing to die.

To the Rain

The rain fell down the length of the Eiffel Tower.
The rain fell the length of every tree on the lawn,
it crossed the desert of every windowpane,
it gave the sun the appearance of a second thought,
it cut the smell of sulphur and the smell of sap,
we were open-gilled and it went right through us.

The clean rain is like the peeling spine, papery,
of an important book title — it comes to mean the day
as words come to mean the things they wrap around,
as I come to mean my love all night in my arms.
The clean rain is a push against the wool blankets,
the unfolding of wings in the City of Light.

And I would ask it if it knows just why it is loved
and where the luck lives in scrap iron, landfill lives,
that the fish should writhe in lethal rapture
to stuff itself with things so small it takes a lifetime,
while this clean rain dents the land, and the sea
shudders from the sharp movements of convulsive breeders.

The Rain Replies

To be a man is to live a topside life, thrust out,
to be forced to breathe air, to swallow and to know
that life no longer passes through you intravenously.
My voice reminds you of the blue inside of the cloud
in which you grew, of a time with closed eyes,
of the nine months you lay in limpidity, creating an island.

If now you ask of the rain, born everywhere at once,
just why it is loved, replies arrive palms-up in the pines,
in columnar mountain springs and slid rivers — just past,
and in the negative of those desert plants which split
red flowers screaming forth in my absence.
I act because I am helpless not to. It brings me love.

Thus, in ten hundred, in Hangzhou, Su Tung-p'o came
to the life on West Lake, with monks and singsong women.
Bear with me, endure me. The boatmen were of two kinds:
those who fed the people, and those who sold their fish
to be thrown back — for such was a way to lay up heavenly treasure.
If caught, the same fish might save three lives from hell.

To an Island

The world isn't pine trees and rain, all pebbles
just small enough to carry the obliquities of the poet
and the odd ironies of the French paragraph-poem.
The rain falls on the food of pigs and dogs,
the evergreen gets its life squeezed out by a set fire,
and the pebble — the pebble is a hand grenade writ small.

They always take away the land where it looks over water.
They have priced it so highly I can barely afford
to live near a tree. The ocean is a receding rumor.

Island known as Long Island, I call on you now
to rise against the rich, to arch your peninsular back
and throw off the cod-like purveyors of private beaches.

Am I angry with nature? No, I love you as I love
my own nature, your body as I love my own. Listen,
you can hear in me the wind that caressed my island
and see in me the shifting dunes and shell-laden tide line.
It is as if a drum were beaten in the streets
far from my island, and I heard an ocean hammering the shore.

The Island Replies

To be a man is to be said no to, principally
by others but occasionally, as now, by oneself.
I am giving you this chance: to leave the Island forever
which in any case is lost to you as a tree is lost
in an unexplored wood. It was your father's island:
his choice, his destination, his finny life-expiring life.

You are a man obsessed with the top twenty-five feet
of the sea, wherein fish swell like bright flags —
fabulous oranges, reds, lavender — and crustaceans appear
to breathe, exhaling an oxidizing powder that bloodies the bottom.
And yet the blueing agency of deep water is most of it below,
as the wind and sand you contain is little more than your skin.

Also, those who scribble about me are little more than sand crabs.
They burrow lightly, and etch lightly, and weigh little.
They are to be honored before the sand sweeps them away.
Is this what you want — to retreat, to be scoured and buried
because you could not bear to leave even one love behind?
Get out of here. Salvage what you can. The rest is imperceptible.

After a Line by Theodore Roethke

In the vaporous gray of early morning,
on the mudflats of the moon, in gray feeling,
walking among boulders uncovered by minus-tides,
I am also still in the still hallway of dream,
facing a stairway without end, in a night without wires,
some recollection hanging in the air, whose image,
unapproachable in the night, waits out there.

Nothing to be gained but rain, and the burning of rain,
this day beginning with such thirst, such capacity
that everything may come to be again in reverse:
a world uncreated, a planet no one is watching —
not even we ourselves — now rising out of misty nothingness,
so that first stones are not solitary nor beings lonely,
nor water divided, nor continents discrete.

Joy to be wordless yet wide awake,
walking by water, in the midst of an unsubstantial suspense,
in clear sight of mist, in mud that sponges up the way back,
in the sight of the closed eyes of one still sleeping,
and there to be gathering shape and form
like a long whip of seaweed being inexorably washed ashore,
and now a head of hair stirring to bring love back which was gone.

Iris of Creation

1990

> *I look at secretive dreams,*
> *I let the straggling days come in,*
> *and the beginnings also, and memories also,*
> *like an eyelid held open hideously*
> *I am watching.*
>
> PABLO NERUDA

He Had a Good Year

while he was going blind. Autumnal light
gave to ordinary things the turning
beauty of leaves, rich with their losing.
A shade of yellow, that once stood opaque
in the rainbow of each glitzy morning,
now became translucent, as if the sun
broke against his own window. As for white,
it was now too much of everything,
as the flat deprivations of the color black
moved farther away: echoes of a surface
unseen and misremembered. I must tell you
how he managed as the lights went slowly out
to look inside the top glow of each object
and make in his mind a spectrum of inner
texture, of an essence isolate from the
nervous trembling of things struck by light.
"Ah, if God were only half the man he is,"
he said, "he would see things this way."

An Old Trembling

Often one wonders what the snake does all day in its pit
to so successfully keep away hands
and be left alone like a solitary zipper
encircling some space from which it has squeezed out all the light
it would seem,
as if no other creature could so love the dark during the day.
And everyone knows about the kiss of the snake.
And everyone knows about the eyes of the snake.
In its mouth is the blue light of old milk.
On its tongue is a map of red rivers.
It knows your body, your own body, like its own.
It begins with your foot, lurking in a boot,
and ends in the venomous sweat of the heart
if you bother it. But whoever leaves alone
whatever in nature wishes not to be disturbed,
he or she will seem like a god,
so unlike a human being,
even to a snake.

Nature

A hand that tries to shake a hand,
an ear pressed against a silver railroad track,
in a place one goes to be alone
called by various names for parts of the body.
Waiting for this, waiting for that.
Swept by the penetrant odor of choked lilies
and the smoke of dark clouds.
Alone by virtue of a garden. And then
with all five senses about to expire,
suddenly a wedding of male and female
in pools of electrochemical memory
that existed before dawn,
before thick and thin, before the dead thought.
Earth of dusk. Earth of the belly. Earth of the breast.
And heaven the heaven of a slash
that wakes the sea.
All that is better, all that is worse,
whatever is half-formed,
which is to say everything born one of two parents,
every living thing turned round in the cave,
unable to distinguish the unlit road
from the bright slash in the sky,
shall be set free to roam
to find a husband or a wife
with whom to ruminate
on the messages in the footprints of ants and flies
and on the rights of others, too, who live
a few hours only or part of a day
without once hearing a rooster
scare away an angel.

Comb and Rake

The comb that we love, of all combs,
is a rake through our private beach,
giving a voice through missing teeth
to all the things one hopes to find in the sand
next to horseshoes, aluminum tabs,
and sand ants thrilled by the sight of a claw.

The rake that we love, of all rakes,
is a comb through our private grove,
singing at perfect intervals
of all the things one hopes to be divine,
here, among human tongues rusting in fire,
bearing the singed hair and beard.

Of all names, the name we most love
mocks an unsaid name we did not love —
in the smallest possible space,
cast upon a screen encircled by a naked moon
at the center of a solar system
where there is only you and me and someone else.

A Man May Change

As simply as a self-effacing bar of soap
escaping by indiscernible degrees in the wash water
is how a man may change
and still hour by hour continue in his job.
There in the mirror he appears to be on fire
but here at the office he is dust.
So long as there remains a little moisture in the stains,
he stands easily on the pavement
and moves fluidly through the corridors. If only one
cloud can be seen, it is enough to know of others,
and life stands on the brink. It rains
or it doesn't, or it rains and it rains again.
But let it go on raining for forty days and nights
or let the sun bake the ground for as long,
and it isn't life, just life, anymore, it's living.
In the meantime, in the regular weather of ordinary days,
it sometimes happens that a man has changed
so slowly that he slips away
before anyone notices
and lives and dies before anyone can find out.

3 Horses Facing the Saskatchewan Sun

They were yellow, brown, golden, tawny.
They were ropy, sinewy, eels in the hands of the three blind men.
They were spirit in the saddle, flesh of belief.
They were posed, they were active, they lived motionless.

Where they stood side by side facing the sun,
where they stood and did not move in the face of the sunshine,
where there they breathed but did not move or twitch,
there they remain in memory and cannot age.

Criminal to tell time to the animals,
brutal to make known one's wish for a change of any kind,
despair to be truthful, cruel to be wishful —
all words to be trampled for the basic right to be.

How He Grew Up

He found the corner of town where the last street
bent, and outdoor lights went down a block
or so and no more. In the long list of states
and their products, there was bauxite, rope,
fire engines, shoes, even a prison, but not one
was famous for purposeless streets and late
walks. Often he missed the truth of lists
while gone for a walk, with most lights out
all over town, and no one told him, when he
returned, the ten things it was best to, or
the dozen it was better not to. He knew
the window would be lit most of the night
down at the camera shop, and the gentle
librarian would keep the house of books open
if he stopped by at closing. Up the street he went,
leaving the lamps, each night until he met
the smell of the bay, a fact to be borne home
to sleep, certain of another day. The houses of
friends were dark. He never told, in those days.
Something was missing from the lists of
best and how to and whose town did what.
He figured, when no other was mentioned,
it might be his town at the top of some list:
but it was hard to read things on paper
in the bony moonlight. So he never knew.
People ask him all the time to have been
where what happened happened, that made
the news, but usually the big things happened
while he was out walking: the War, the War, etc.

I, or Someone Like Me

In a wilderness, in some orchestral swing
through trees, with a wind playing all the high notes,
and the prospect of a string bass inside the wood,
I, or someone like me, had a kind of vision.
As the person on the ground moved, bursting halos
topped first one tree, then another and another,
till the work of sight was forced to go lower
into a dark lair of fallen logs and fungi.

His was the wordless death of words, worse
for he remembered exactly where the words were
on his tongue, and before that how they fell
effortlessly from the brainpan behind his eyes.
But the music continued and the valley of forest floor
became itself an interval in a natural melody
attuned to the wind, embedded in the bass of boughs,
the tenor of branches, the percussion of twigs.

He, or someone like him, laughed at first,
dismissing what had happened as the incandescence
of youthful metabolism, as the slight fermentation
of the last of the wine, or as each excuse of love.
Learning then the constancy of music and of mind,
now he takes seriously that visionary wood
where he saw his being and his future underfoot
and someone like me listening for a resolution.

Portrait

1

Without the lightness of the sponge,
without the armor of the clam,
without a look about a ship
at rest on the bottom,
without so much in the sight of eternity,
of which these pictures are but samples.

2

With bare knuckles,
with many trees felled,
with many times in the bottom of the rowboat
pressing my hands equally
toward port and starboard
as the great cruisers swamped us.

3

With the flickering of stars,
with melodies improvised
on a framework of space,
with intervals, with distances to run,
with a God who is the breeze
around my fire.

4

And a bruise in the water,
and swift current,
and half a loaf,
and the zero of the sun,
and a skewed body
and an iron kiss.

5

Among shards of gourds.
In the roar of the pine sap.
With the carcass of a sparrow
and the banner of the dew.
In a smear of history.
In the thrill of a green flash.

Tall Ships

The one who reaches the crow's nest
has to go by way of a boot full of water,
wearing a long rope burn and blue tattoos,
and drinking a bucketful of salt,
and always with an eye big enough to let in a star.

The one who reaches the crow's nest has to go
by the path of most resistance,
leaving the deck behind with childhood wishes
and climbing from the wide life of floors
to the narrow end of the telescope filled by a moon.

The one who reaches the crow's nest absolutely
must want to, rehearsing in dreams
the layout of cat's cradles and spider webs,
forgetting all ordinances and averages,
apathetic to the widening embrace of the planets.

The one who reaches the crow's nest,
the one who tops the mast and the crow's nest,
has to go up by way of the two hands of a pulley,
by following the fists of the clock to noon,
and by turning his face to the blind dial of the cosmos.

An Elegy for the Past

It will be darker soon, colder. You see
the corner where you will turn, and you
turn. The house you think is yours,
the door, wait in shadow to be chosen,
and you choose them, and enter, and slowly
peel the layers off that held close an extra
part of the world: the one you entered when
your planet suddenly expanded. Someone
died, and then the universe seemed larger.
Earth swung a sickle path around the sun.
You saw it all in your mind, apart. You were
quiet, and everything was time. All you had
to do was wait, and everything was time.

I Will Not Be Claimed

When I am happy, nothing can divide me
against myself, and I will not be owned.
The carnation in the buttonhole above my head
passes me and I do not look up to see who.
The armored truck parks by the coffee shop
and I do not notice how many the money bags are.
Even the rapturous smell of a new perfume
reaches me but I do not look up to beauty.

When I am happy, truly happy, nothing
can separate me and I will not be claimed.
I cling to the grass and will not let it go
and the threats of winter do not convince me.
I linger over the last of the bread and coffee
and I do not notice the cook locking his doors.
The bad news and the books about death
are part of what we live for, when I am happy.

But when I am not happy, I am one of those
who is broken down into parts and stopped.
I am the brain of a human being but not a being.
I am the heart of a man but not that man.
I see the cook closing and it feels like the end.
Whether I am to be happy or unhappy, I see
which it will be as of the morning, after waking.
I see the white stuff and the black stuff and decide.

By the Iowa

I think I lived among the currents of a river
without recognizing the groove it made in sky
because it was the habit of men in a family way
not to follow a tide out or a current away
over to what would surely be an unprotected falls
in the days before all cliffs were flagged upstream.

This river found its length and width in ice
when the famous glacier parked and sank through soil
black for ways of looking that had work to do
and the kinds of rules that draft horse hooves
impress along the course of what a field can gain
when land becomes hometown, the lessons and the days.

Deer turn away from the shallows of this river
that runs out of a wilderness toward a skyline
where even low roofs promise an appetite for rain
awkward for self-sufficient men to wish for helplessly
but muskrat venture with owls and bats
and the catfish come to be by a whisker of evolution.

These banks are what the outside of a curve is
and these bridges are for walking on the water
and these rocks are in the river to originate
new soil somewhere in a well-fed century
this side of glaciers when crops may grow in sand
dry to purpose but patient for success.

That future too records its look on eggshells
ground into the route some new river may run
over these places I peer today to catch my look
in deep surfaces that steadily look back at me
while the river rinses off with upstream water
that began in ice before there was any feeling.

Dark Brow

The dark brow of the creek wrinkles over time
as if something had been born there.
Scavenging all night, the water that runs there
brings things from time past.
Some of these things are the wrappers, the coats,
of what it meant to say "I tasted"
or "I felt." And this, whatever it is, is not that.

All of us have felt the fatigue of dark water,
the burden massed at yard's edge,
and in the line of the garden
beyond the onions, there are fresh tears.
I do not say we should live forever,
for who could bear it,
only that we should one day enter completely into life.

In the beginning, as at the end, there was nothing,
though "was" is the psychic's verb,
the one that proves the existence of a current
by rising after it has passed
and shaking its head furiously, spraying water.
"I was," we say. "Therefore, I am." We also believe
a piece of us has washed away and may be worth something.

A Primer About the Flag

Or certain ones. There are Bed & Breakfast flags.
They fly over vacancies, but seldom
above full houses. Shipboard, the bridge can say
an alphabet of flags. There are State flags
and State Fair flags, there are beautiful flags
and enemy flags. Enemy flags are not supposed
to be beautiful, or long-lasting. There are flags
on the moon, flags in cemeteries, costume flags.
There are little flags that come from the barrel
of a gun and say, "Bang." If you want to have
a parade, you usually have to have a flag
for people to line up behind. Few would
line up behind a small tree, for example,
if you carried it at your waist just like a flag
but didn't first tell people what it stood for.

Icarus Thought

The nature of a circle prevents it
from ever being a human hand.
And the essence of a rectangle
prevents it from ever being a skull.
Yet important people who can see
for themselves can't get this straight.
So others have to give them a picture
of the moon burning inside a mouth
and worms nesting within a cloud
and an empty sleeve that screams.

One who knows the hollows of a skull
will have felt the remorse of a knife.
And one who truly sees the moon
will know the sadness of the twilight.
But that fool we were in wax,
he will be lifted always by emptiness
and made to embrace the music,
first of the sun and then of the moon,
and learn the ambivalence of doorways
and a dawn that looks like evening.

Washing Our Hands of the Rest of America

The water is moving again in the lakes of Central America.
On the surface it is peaceful, but at the bottom
the smallest things move about: sand grains, pebbles,
creatures the bulk of a single human hair
with stomachs the size of follicles.
These are the fingers of the deep effects:
when a body disappears into the water,
shifting ground and brainless flitting things
rub away the guilt and responsibility. Soon enough,
the lake water is fit again for drinking
and the laundry of creatures with the bulk of locomotives
and stomachs the size of bomb craters. Someone writes
to the newspaper to express his anger:
"Nothing is clean. The water here, which was pure,
can no longer be digested. The lake nauseates me.
The doctors say that I am allergic to my own brain.
No, I am allergic to the brains of those who run things.
I am going away now. I will live at home.
You will see me as always, but I will have gone away.
The only thing now is not to disappear."

If I Had One Thing to Say

I see words effaced in the footprints of the conquered,
slowly sinking into the earth in a round sort
of way, indirect, like sunlight at night, and I see
the speeches of the conquerors preserved on paper,
hurried to a lead mine in the mountains and buried
deeper than atomic mushrooms, insulated
from firestorm and radiation and residue even if
the world has to wait ten thousand years for Adam.

I see grass growing rapidly in those footprints,
and the earth curving in space, and the lean of all
that holds on, from the laughter of the lone coyote
high up in the night to the wishbone of the kill,
hung head down to drain and every part used
and remembered as long as song, deep as prayer,
with the words handed down through centuries
of naming and telling and there's always another Adam.

I see dust made of the fibers of grass, of paper,
from the rubbings of the dirt, the pumice of dead bone,
from the cells of our skin migrating to the surface,
and I see that the dust will never settle, neither
in time nor space, but in the rain of a thousand centuries
many things clear now to us — impulses at the core —
may come to rest in the form of a thought, and this
may be the way it is already: the way it was for Adam.

Sevens (Version 3): In the Closed Iris of Creation

A pair of heavy scissors lay across the sky
waiting for an affirmation,
waiting for the go-ahead of tragic love.
The sky, as always, was full of sobbing clouds
ready to rain down heavily on desire
wherever a hand opens or a leg stretches out
and life waits to begin —
the way everything, even scissors, waits to begin.
We who began in water, in clay,
in the ancient diggings of the word,
whitened by the chalk of dreams,
bloom in colors (everyone has noticed!)
blind toward scissors and clouds.
Within the sight of a pail of water,
our mothers pushed us away
for the good of our souls
into a world where the sun had burned a hole
in the name of love.
Now sleep in the sewers
descends, bringing us an inner life
at peace behind an in-turning iris —
crawling, pre-cadaverous, fetal.
To choose between knowing the truth
or, on the other hand, orgasm and repose,
always like a cricket on guard
in case Spring should arrive in disguise,
hiding its muscular body under rags,
its footsteps muffled by the mating of vines —
to choose at all, we have to crawl
on bare knees down alleys of pumice
and plead among the red columns of silos,
in the dust of exploding grains,
with shaking hands and trembling lips

plead for a severing of the knives.
If now in the black hole we sometimes dance
like orphans among new loaves of bread,
and lift plain water to toast
our good luck, and if in a thicket of almonds
bearing the smell of oil before it turns
to bitter wine,
we laugh so hard we lose our bodies momentarily,
we are also, at the same time, absorbing
the shivering of the cities
born of this baked earth, this chaste diamond
that flowered, reluctantly, absurdly,
into an eternity of ice
and descended through the decorations of the frost
to be shipwrecked in space.
Thus, each morning I throw a little chalk into my coffee
in memory of the blood and bones of the universe,
and each day I eat some sacramental bread
as a prayer
not to become one of the thieves
but to save and keep my life for whenever I may need it,
perhaps when things are going better,
when everything is or isn't sevens,
and the planet is in perpetual motion
giving continuous birth to the space behind her.
I myself swear never to be surprised
when someone tries to stay in the womb.
The great silence that filled the Void
was grounded by the first rain,
beaten into piles of grain and no grain
in the first silo, in the first air,
without a place to put a foot down, without an us,
all in a hole

that held (aloft? upside down?) as if in an iris
the thin tracings of the first wax,
and of the first delicate amoebic embracings,
and of the shapes to come when love
began to sever us.

Darts

The way the feathers follow the tip of the dart
is the way we can be when the wind's up. To the
docks to tie up the boats, if it's a hurricane,
but once in a while a story begins and a path
changes because a little breeze arrived,
from the howl of a baby, from an open door.

The way of the steel point leading the feathers
is the way we have been in still air. To the
yard to water the lawn, if it's a drought,
but once in a while a lifetime occurs and a door
reopens because a ripping-down wind is born
from the cry of a victim, from a barred window.

The days are not our target, nor the nights.
Wildly and without care, things have no end,
but once in a while when we reach out a hand
something in the air will come take hold of it,
and drag us along, spiraling out of control,
and drop us just as quickly when we let go.

Victim of Himself

He thought he saw a long way off the ocean
cresting and falling, bridging the continents,
carrying the whole sound of human laughter
and moans — especially moans, in the mud of misery —
but what he saw was already diluted, evaporating,
and what he felt were his teeth grinding
and the bubbles of saliva that broke on his tongue.

He was doomed to be a victim of himself.
He thought he saw, in the future, numberless, cavernous
burials — the outcome of plagues, of wars,
of natural disasters created by human beings —
but what he saw was already faded, disintegrating,
and what he felt was the normal weakness displayed
by droopy eyes and muscles that bleated meekly.

He thought he saw from Earth up to the stars
and from any one moment back to the hour of his birth
when desire produced, in the slush of passionate tides,
a citizen of mud and ash, of lost light and dry beds,
but what he saw was already distorted, moving away,
and what he felt was a sense of loss that so often
he had been at peace in her arms when he did not intend to be.

Poem After Carlos Drummond de Andrade

"It's life, Carlos."

It's life that is hard: waking, sleeping, eating, loving, working and
  dying are easy.
It's life that suddenly fills both ears with the sound of that
   symphony that forces your pulse to race and swells your
   heart near to bursting.
It's life, not listening, that stretches your neck and opens your eyes
   and brings you into the worst weather of the winter to
   arrive once more at the house where love seemed to be in
   the air.

And it's life, just life, that makes you breathe deeply, in the air that
   is filled with wood smoke and the dust of the factory,
   because you hurried, and now your lungs heave and fall
   with the nervous excitement of a leaf in spring breezes,
   though it is winter and you are swallowing the dirt of
   the town.
It isn't death when you suffer, it isn't death when you miss each
   other and hurt for it, when you complain that isn't death,
   when you fight with those you love, when you
   misunderstand, when one line in a letter or one remark in
   person ties one of you in knots, when the end seems near,
   when you think you will die, when you wish you were
   already dead — none of that is death.
It's life, after all, that brings you a pain in the foot and a pain in the
   hand, a sore throat, a broken heart, a cracked back, a torn
   gut, a hole in your abdomen, an irritated stomach, a
   swollen gland, a growth, a fever, a cough, a hiccup, a
   sneeze, a bursting blood vessel in the temple.
It's life, not nerve ends, that puts the heartache on a pedestal and
   worships it.

It's life, and you can't escape it. It's life, and you asked for it. It's life,
and you won't be consumed by passion, you won't be
destroyed by self-destruction, you won't avoid it by
abstinence, you won't manage it by moderation, because
it's life — life everywhere, life at all times — and so you
won't be consumed by passion: you will be consumed
by life.

It's life that will consume you in the end, but in the meantime...
It's life that will eat you alive, but for now...
It's life that calls you to the street where the wood smoke hangs,
and the bare hint of a whisper of your name, but before
you go...

Too late: Life got its tentacles around you, its hooks into your heart,
and suddenly you come awake as if for the first time, and
you are standing in a part of the town where the air is
sweet — your face flushed, your chest thumping, your
stomach a planet, your heart a planet, your every organ a
separate planet, all of it of a piece though the pieces turn
separately, O silent indications of the inevitable, as among
the natural restraints of winter and good sense, life blows
you apart in her arms.

Initial Conditions

The way the sun will slant,
breaking through the window of the Uptown Café
to light a page from Dickinson or Moore,
may pick up the names of America's presidents
as they appear on street signs —
Lincoln, Lawrence, Clay, Franklin, Jefferson,
Washington and then Water Street —
to imbue history with artistry,
and that, in the spotlight of a metabolic fire
born of solitude in the midst of crowds,
may flatten the raised fibers of ten blank pages.
Black where there was white, and ink
where there was water, is the current on which rides
the deep guttural imagination of the animal,
the ethereal silence of the plant,
the indifferent face of the stone and the dirt
and the bittersweet knowledge of a man or woman
buried in ecstasy the way light flies from fire.

Have your bacon and eggs, have your toast.
Simmer again the early pinpricks of sensation:
those wordless turns in the amniotic river,
the ballooning, the shaping, the reaching,
and then the glare, the hands,
the separation and all the half-returns and afternoons.
Swell again toward the little world of the child.
Sit on your hands, now,
the adult who can still feel from fingertip inward.
Mark how it feels on the bench. Note the air
cool in May as it mummifies briefly and moves on.
Live at the end of your nose,
on the outskirts of the balls of your eyes,
at the purge of your mouth. Push out your stomach

as you breathe, let your chest sag to feel bone.
The kneecap that moves like a seashell,
the elastic and the inelastic upper leg —
tuck a leg under your chair.

It is all a spine, from which the leaves of the tree
seem to ask for applause,
and round which the breathing of all life-forms
distributes seasons and light. It is ever
a spine distributing the shiver of a ghost
who comes to float from out the fog
these islands, spits, peninsulas and continents.
At the spine-tip end of a leaf
a momentary flame spits from the veins,
the same as the sun sends out a green flash as it dives,
and as the brain may flare
at the end of a spinal message, keeping
in mind every pony stop up the long vertebrae
of calcified civilization,
yet still at the tip end of the earth,
at the farthest reach of a root,
find water in the white dust, and blood in an old stain,
enough to bear the future in the air.

Be your weight. Take your smallest step
from word one, build your home at one o'clock,
when the big hand sweeps it away, build at two, at three
and so on, no more ahead of time than that.
Where grease has touched the corner
of a page, it travels edge to edge, erasing opacity.
Be like oil, sometimes like sand or fire,
blown about but unbroken,
stuff that offers hope to the coughing engine

and the fouled shore and the frozen.
Watch the honeybee, how little it takes away,
and how many times it returns
for the necessity of a queen. You are the bee,
if you are a poet at all, eloping with nectar,
proposing honey, and leaving it stamped into a matrix
of wax, in swarming and smoke to grow old.
I read a page in the café, and read the same again,
and then it begins to grow in size and sweetness.

Now, everyone wants to know about failure.
Mankind likes to come upon the bones of the sparrow
or the flattened hide on the highway,
and return to it as a student of entropy,
noting the white salts that have come to the surface,
the caves eaten by insects, the plucked eyeball.
But I say learn your successes.
Unbend from your studies, let the wind in from the west,
and stay your prayers another hour.
In that hour, that indolence, that dreaming,
an angel may salute you,
the sign of which is a rush of responses
to some small thing on the earth, to which you are noon
on the sundial. In a burst, you must get them out
if there is to be peace, if there is to be
completion, if there is to be the road ahead
which we are all traveling, because love can rub its eyes
and even read the paw marks at road's edge.

I have lingered over a page,
recording in wrongly shaped letters Americans
going to work on the noisy streets of cars and cranes,
footsoles scraping to hurry, calling out,

electric switches clicking on at the corner
and old neon signs in windows buzzing to expire,
until the last door closed and an arc of silence
hooded the abandoned outdoors.
I appealed to myself not to make food from poison
or blood from water or song from interval,
but to loiter in the vacancy,
waiting for a signal, an inkling, of truth,
and I never had to wait long,
because sooner or later the most horrible things happened
somewhere that brought an ambulance
and a man running down the street carrying flowers
which only a moment's thought could tell me
were too early for a death and must be something else.

And after the refueling, what then?
After the regeneration, with the fog easing upward
from the prone earth into a dissolving embrace,
and the tide turning tail, its last
washing down the mudflats where penlights of air
sent to the surface by living remains
flicker in a constellation too hurried for pictures.
What of the shark's teeth underfoot?
How goes the tide line of beached seaweed
back to the water? Sit still and see.
Stay at your post, your bridal window into the new day,
resist the urge to begin again, to alter even your shadow,
and so to witness a world unaffected by self.
Steel yourself against the delusion at the bottom
of the cup, where the grounds of coffee
may speak in the shape of a dial. It is not a direction
to be at the center of the compass, nor will you be
revealed by wrapping yourself in glass.

If it were not for words, poor words,
I would never have known the wish that things continue.
Let pleasure continue and pain, and bread
and milk continue to spoil, and erosion
go on as before at the joining of wind and rock
and even where a blade of grass shoulders the road.
Let the apple lose its grip in oversweetness
and the honey settle into layers.
All that falls to the ground to be absorbed
may be confused with death, painted with sad tones,
without a thought for the joy of pure pity
or the painter swept by a ghostly excitement.
Each one of us believes he or she keeps watch,
while in reality we are watched. Each of us
believes we are dying, while in reality we live.
Each of us falls into the trap, tearing away
at the sphere which protects and regenerates us,
the one best described by a pirouette or a cartwheel.

And so the wandering canine knows, the mutt,
knows how a hand may curl into a fist,
or the fist unfold, intuits when the meal ends
and leftovers begin, and remembers the doors of largesse
up lanky alleys to the chimney walls of kitchens.
Walk then with such a dog in town, and with the cat,
the one who parallels your nightly reconnoitering
until you stop and squat, surrendering
to its benign approach. How the independent world
loves that which breathes and yet is still,
like the cat, and will rub at the chance of quick love,
cajoling your shoe and trouser cuff,
arching with half a question, perhaps this one:
"Would you, if I...?" and purring like the underside

of a wave that might have slid inexorably through a dream.
It is a dream to be a human being, cast here among
the dreamless days of cats and dogs,
carrying the burden of their mute imagination.

By animal methods, no need to deny,
and only by animal methods, we have understood
the timelessness of our lives. By sexuality,
we have unlaced the proper shoetops, the stitched waters
of history, and then the lines of entanglement,
the cuneiforms of emotions, the ciphers of agreements,
and found there is a flavor, an odor,
a hope on the edge of uncontainable sensation,
a taste of blissful agony, poised on the head of a pin,
emanating from our bones, a singing wire —
that tight, that tense, that stretched to its limit
and then shattered — the ends pulled apart
now limitless in the distance spreading between them,
the torn tips of the last exposed fibers
splayed, letting go, catching each other as they fall,
creating random sparks that fall to the ground
like bits and pieces of some lost moronic code
staggering, exhausted, into the future.

The report we await goes well beyond the outer rim,
leaping like the vague shape of climax
past the short grasses at the edge of the bluff
that appears after heavy exertion
as an unseen clarity, the sure feeling that if one opened
one's eyes, and screamed, there would be a limit,
a panel, a backdrop to mark the event. So much have we
been certain, that much have we been pulled
by the next horizon, and the next,

leaving echo after echo. The report we await
is yours to make from the bottom of time,
from the place behind the last, narrowed bits of light,
where sound sucks up sound, the corporeal
equivalent, the adult version of what the child knew
who tumbled into the well, and lay for days
underneath the big story, being of households and news
but to itself the absence of the world
into which it would again be born someday, unabandoned.

If it were not so, memory would serve.
But we have found nothing, and science likewise,
to locate presences of life in long fibers of ink
carried by a heart, nor in the lengthy recitation
of presidents engraved within a street plan, nor in a flair
for the names of battles or the dates of books or even
in a penchant for destinations and right answers.
Deaf Beethoven in his last quartet better serves.
Where is it, that such sound ends in clarity and calm?
Is it in the mind, in the heart, in the stomach,
in the liver, the reproductive organs, the limbs?
Is it in the pulse and travels through us? Is it on the skin,
absorbing and radiating, warming and chilling? And, too,
how have we known the feeling — sitting, listening?
Such questions are like a harbor of twilights.
They lead us into the valley of unanswerable nights.
They decline, they evade, they ride at anchor
beyond the reach of the pier, a harp to the wind.

Memory is pre-history. Remember, if you can,
the net into which you fell in the pre-conscious dawn,
its gridwork, arrayed along a horizontal figure 8.
The whole of it is here today, in this historical town.

Condense your past, squeeze recurrent dreams,
and look also among the residues of dirt and water,
in the lingering odor of fresh bread, in mold,
and in that which drifts your way from rumor
and idea, from under the forehead of abstractions,
those thunderous proclamations of the mind's eye.
In little words is sewn an elemental red thread
that holds together old shoes and new philosophies,
cats and dogs, the first and last steps of a stairway,
the careful fugitive and the accidental isolate.
All that was is here, pouring into this moment,
which offers you every chance for tears. But forget,
if you can, all that has gone through the mystic's cloth,
and spot what disturbs the air with heavy laughter.

Hear it in the cathedral burned into a redwood,
in the fluid gear turning the beacon
at the top of the lighthouse, its light bobbing above
thirteen miles of fog and tidal signatures. See it,
when you can, in the filmy stem of Indian pipe,
devout to fungi but deathly when plucked,
though it takes a day or more to gain that burnt look.
After the blaze that rode the trees and seemed
to keep the sky at bay, in the fresh death of the muck,
legions of fireweed strode the blackened soil,
throwing their youth out while the old ones slept.
You live because a glacier melts, a forest dies,
an animal somewhere falls to its knees,
and you would see in the night face of the owl
a feline curiosity, independent in judgment,
quietly paying out the night to survive. Once again
night's force has unraveled, its harpoon
lying in a vague acreage of water after feeding.

So many follow the weather, and rehearse it,
riding an impending high like vacationers
and wallowing in crusty lows like bean farmers.
Standing out at dusk, sweeping the last solar wink
over the horizon, throwing back our heads
to fit — lens and shutter — up against the concave
camera obscura overhead, we let go, finally, if only
we stay to look up, the false evidence of edges
and distances where once the commonest objects fit.
Where now does an umbrella belong, or a coat?
The weight of a machine tilts it absurdly
underneath the violent ramshackle orders of a galaxy.
Now the explosion at the heart of a star
walks the beams of the past, now a fiery arrow
rounds the curve, braiding itself in flame. But a rose
might be pictured where a single thread expires,
and the whole head of a flowering mountain ash
turns out to be a nest of stars at a low level of heat.

Miraculous to be alive in a tungsten universe,
to count the windows and change our point of view
according to their shape and location, and ourselves
as well, marked in secret by the birth of each idea,
welcome to men and women but not all,
revising and refuting our gods, burning in the fall,
but first gathering the leaves, and then irresistibly
flinging ourselves into the piles,
sometimes having to do it at the length of the rake
because men and women must fast more than children
to reach the next meal, and because of such things
as give each person a feeling
for the souls of those who knew kisses but few words,
and those who said little but laughed easily,

and some who trembled from the beginning to the end
as if they were connected at both ends
to opposing charges and were fated to be incinerated
where others carried torches with impunity.

When the time comes that you walk inside a cloud,
where others may sense but not see you,
and you as clear to yourself as ever, charitable
to the lack of visibility, adoring the fog, silencing
desire, flinging your sense of yourself from guidance,
lingering in the great freedom of invisibility,
then inevitably the cloak burns,
and you may be told not to walk on the grass.
The wilderness of the mind comes down to a ranger,
a file of pressed flowers arranged by color,
and the deer who crowd from the trees to lick
the antifreeze of automobiles. When you were inside
the cloud, and your feet rocked slightly with each step
on the watery land, were you (tell us) as alone
with your eyes open as ever you had been asleep?
Here then is a use for the blows of a pencil-point
against the grain of a page. At impact, a purity
is born from the attraction and repulsion of an instant.

One must be fond of the mud road, of boats
with names that itch to flaunt the pulse that wrote them,
of beachcombers, of detectives gone to birding,
of the beautiful handles of hand tools, of dropped coins,
of propellers and sudden rainbows, of distant ice fields
and glacial streams, of tide pools, of house pets,
of gardens and clotheslines and mint weed by doorsteps.
One must be fond of these things,
as of empty churches and old schoolyards in long grass,

because love, even light love, reaches back
and picks up what others held, one way or another,
long after a dig is emptied of pots and bones and teeth.
Out of such fondness, the telling. The blaze
of a face that would tell us washes the yellow light
of after-midnight, the conversation continues,
and the table spreads to include long-missing friends,
presidents, explorers, those who left or returned,
who have not been deserted, whether or not they know.

To be located, as here, at the table of one's examples,
to have for the moment the unmasked,
the everyday, and all of it having slept in the dark,
diving near a dream reef with as many handholds
as a sponge has openings, and where easily
one might have stood fatally upon the dreaded stonefish
or been poisoned from being hauled up too quickly —
these then are one's "particulars." I know,
time has overtaken the deciduous, as night again
will paralyze the open eye, and our sodium streetlights
will rub and rub the open wounds, the doomsdays,
the little edge that pebbles give to the sound of steps
and spittle gives to song. I know,
all this too will pass, and may have passed already,
but still I address you where last you were seen
and, whether or not you understood chaos
or sensitive dependence, whether or not you felt
the synchronicity of our lives, there is no one else to.

Drink what remains of your coffee, close your book.
Is it possible that we no longer see ourselves
reflected in open theaters,
no longer exist by the grace of lowered cannon

or can be said to have vanished
because a cloud came, or a fog, or death? Let it
now be decided if the rain must be too heavy
for the certainty of charity. Or if we are made of ash.
Or if sufferance has blistered its skin of paint
on the sides of unconquerable mountains. The moon
that drew us to its scent, only to be faceless,
is the cache of our romance, but also a truth that spills
into the faults of the mind, depositing a dewy light
where the shapes of animals, living and extinct,
hover in some wounded swamp from which,
when we fully awake, we see the imagination rising,
cloud-like, slowly lifting and thinning out,
resembling a gifted child's version of a ghost.

Spring–Summer, 1989
Port Townsend, Washington

FROM

A Marvin Bell Reader

1994

One must imagine Sisyphus happy.

ALBERT CAMUS

Ecstasy

And there are cries, muffled, from a closed room,
and there is that kind of rough argument
that sounds like the tussling of a tiger and a stuffed bear,
and there is, in the moist lines of a lover's hand,
a narrative of need and desire
and the brief story of two who meet and instantly
know the full measure of their breathing,
each enlarged by the other's,
until the door falls open to let out the old cries,
and the argument is overcome by one ravaging swipe
of the tiger's claws, and they are set loose.

All the sorrow in the world
attends the bed where two find happiness,
and they will rise to it, bleached and drained, afterward,
but now there are only legs like none other,
and hands and mouths like never before, and sensations
impossible before this moment, this dream.
In this feverish circle, which moves and does not move
at once, in this updraft of overweening feeling,
in this constant approach to the cliff
of afterward, the lovers burn with reality,
and are emptied of it, and say they are happy.

There are natural limits to what may be known
about another, and the testing of it
is scored at night in the pipelines of tenements,
in vibrations on the surface of pooled water,
and in the personal thermostats of comfort
by those who close or open their eyes without blinking,
by those who toss and turn without restlessness,
and by those who shiver in fever and burn in cold.
You don't want to know this, unless you are so engaged,

how the lover craves more, openly,
how the lovers glue themselves together to be broken.

Without words, everything may be known at once.
Sing or scream, be light or heavy,
be utterly aware from the adrenaline of her desire
or dizzy from the accumulations of surrender,
you will feel it in the protruding parts of the body
as always, but then, if this is to be the true wreckage,
you will feel it in the in-turning areas,
there at the waist, in the creases and hollows,
at the neck, at the hinges of the wrist and knee,
in the curled-up sole of each foot, under
the drawn-in tongue, behind the lips, and in a line

that passes through the solar plexus. Explode now,
you are the world, you did not do this alone.
Bite your life in two, let the high frequencies
of your screams speak for you and the low level
of your moaning be the planet's undercurrent.
These are life, what you must come back to,
though it be closeted in public
as if it were to be doubted, or feared.
In bed, in arousal, in a savage sensitivity,
there the high fury of lovers feels eternal
as they fall and fall through the spray into now.

When it is over, you may strangle the bedside flowers.
When it is over, you may cut through the web
of that spider whom you protected and observed
at the doorway — for now is the cold at the window.
Akimbo, the lovers find themselves. Akimbo,
spun out from the center, cast nerve lengths

from that red coal withdrawing in the fire pit
which a thundershower has doused —
akimbo, the lovers gather themselves now
for the long climb up from the chasm. Others
said it was a human sacrifice — their friends come

to a perilous edge, and indeed a volcanic cauldron
simmered at the base. They themselves
simmered and burned and simmered some more,
and cooled, and now the climb needs handholds,
and one hoists oneself by tiny purchases
in sheets and coverlets, pushing off from the resistance
of aching springs and loosened headboards,
shaking free of a dampness, making for the high edge
where one first viewed the chaos like a visitor.
At the bluff, the high weeds have wilted,
exposing the beaten squares where blankets lay.

Dizzily, we look back and step away. Dizzily, we surge
out of the beloved, pushing aside our embrace,
and twist to see beyond a shoulder if any remain
of the last sparks and fire trails, whatever they were
at the base of the brain. Already nothing may be left
but a murmur of residual warmth as it rises,
like us, to mix with the hours an odd light-headedness,
the source of which eludes and eludes us
as we dress again and concentrate on the days ahead.
Walk, now, as far as you like on shaky legs.
This place you found is not a room and has no exit.

How many plan to die while making love
and pay into every wishing well that the days ahead
resemble the past, that once, that burned? Confess,

student of smell, scholar of the kinetic nuance,
confess that, among all the creatures of the world,
men and women alone must thrash or resist
to reach pure feeling. And there are middles to stories,
and there are insects that click by, and flies
that simmer as they die in the candy of the spider web,
suspended, and there is the moment when the lovers
rip into the silence, to quiet it with their cries.

Short Version of Ecstasy

Up-welling of forces, serums and fevers,
tracking conduits of emotion,
following the longing of waist, elbows and knees
to crease to and fro, to be wind and wild
as any petal of in-growing rosebud in storm.
Until, and not until, each still quivering tendon
flops its last and pales;
until, and not until, something of a trance or sleep
blankets the bed; until, and not until, a dozen instances
lift and collapse in a headless consciousness
of release, and the gorged blood descends
by an intermittent elevator of stems,
will the lovers let go of themselves or each other.

Can they stand to get up now? So far have they slid
from the inflated lungs of love,
from the gasping expectation and the drag
of skin on skin as they sank after having held up
their coming, they who moved as one
raw from the separate rates of their falling,
such a distance have they gone, up and down then,
that each may recall the middle of the story
only by its frame. After the event,
the photo of the lover expels no scent, no invitation
sufficient to satisfy. It is truly over until,
and only until, some hidden residue of passion
sways into being, wanting to die.

Cryptic Version of Ecstasy

To have been a rose among white poppies,
to have opened to the delirium
that each day shatters the night on all sides
and at night pulls down upon itself the day,
and to have scrubbed the dripping wall
from the inside out, writhing with the labors
of harsh pleasure, to have felt one might
surely burst without again catching one's life
as it rose and dipped and vanished —
is to have been wooed and won.

And to have had a place to be streaming,
to have ridden the tossing vacancies
that lend the days their view from above
and the nights their plummeting echoes,
and to have turned the misshapen rod
from the outside in, pressing with the effort
of rough elation, to have known the moment
when the blooming occurs, like blood
among porcelain figurines — such is the prize
of true love, or so it was given me to say.

Eastern Long Island

Beach grass tangled by wind — the sound rushes
to every nautical degree —
here are torn memories of inlets and canals,
of ponds, bays, creeks, coves, spits and sandbars,
coastal moons and skies, tidal clumps of tiny crabs
that couldn't keep up, seaweed fixed
to stones looking like the heads of Chinese sages,
all crisscrossing the sundial of my dreams.

I dream more when the meteors come —
Earth's face slipping through a comet's tail —
reminder that we steer an unmarked channel,
buoyless, sounding the vacancy of space
where water turns
to take back what it said and deposit on the shore
the exhausted sailor, his tired, complaining boat,
and the wrack of saltwater pouring through the slats.

Wasn't anything to be done. Where ships foundered,
where pilgrims settled and pioneers set off,
now contaminant plumes propose
marriage to the aquifer, this being the way it was
when the shark lost teeth to the incoming tide,
and those legs that covet the tide line
were torn from the armored, methodical crab,
and the gull grabbed off the fish closest to the top.

Wasn't anything to be done — not then
when rapture simmered underwater, and we played
adulthood, taking sea horse and starfish,
nor later when the fishermen
followed their catch to deeper water,
leaving a stain that coated rocks and weeds

and seemed to be of a shade containing
its own shadow, an undulation in the channel.

Time has not ended. Yet already it is a struggle
to brush away the first few flecks
starlight lent this crystalline surface, then mute.
Earth's voice, a harmony begun in molten rumble,
rose through wash of water and rush of air
to the high pitch of grass blade and ether light.
Those first bits of impurity, that were to ruin
our diamond in the making, at first barely marked it.

I still love the radiance of a dim storm building
out where the tide seems to reverse and the sea vibrate,
puzzling perhaps to fresh eyes yet unfazed
by salt wells rising beneath these beds of clay.
At the tide line a fringe of seaweed keeps time,
and wind-whipped sand opaques our cottage windows.
By the boat ramp, disgorged clamshells await
reclamation by the proximate meek, who shall inherit.

Poem in Orange Tones

Curtains hung closed, sealing off the window,
and the silver waste of a snail glistened
on the sidewalk outside, minutely rotting,
where night had taken its fluttering light away
and a rumbling in the world's belly
signaled the rising red of a day. Dew trembled
to keep its balance on a spear of grass.
Dirt lamented in the cemeteries. The fir
grieved not to be as hard as oak or olive.
Everything in the world regretted something —
the ash not to be fire, blue not to be red,
a radish not to have the smell of an onion.
Thus, with the whole world resisting waking up,
men and women, also, woke
slowly, reluctantly, with eyelashes melted together
and frozen brows
and would have tossed all day long in bed
like fallen leaves
if certain trees had not produced a sound like laughter,
if particular birds had not sung in orange tones,
or if the air had not wrecked itself
on the lower lip of the horizon. A white journey
was beginning, rosy in the distance,
a drone was starting to sound just under the surface
of the land, in the woods where it had been too wet
to echo and in the water, now that the moon
had stopped pulling
orphaned questions out of private prayers,
and it was time. The doors opened.
The curtains spread. What if there was to be rage
in the middle of metal, rebellion in some motor
somewhere, or wrath in the weather?
Whatever can happen will, and rakes will clatter

to clear the consequence of time,
and saws will sing to fell even the olive tree,
and the strength of the onion falter,
but still we live the days
as if in a crystal
in which the smell of fruit is increased
day by day by the sun.
And the color yellow regrets it was never green,
and the east and the west long to trade places,
and the shadow would like just once
to come out on top.

Interview

Do you believe that actors are dumb? Writers?

Which of the following do you think are the dumbest: actors, writers, policemen, firemen, hunters, or generals?

How about social workers, teachers, doctors, realtors?

Fat people, prisoners, the poorly dressed, the visibly impoverished?

The sick, the old, the lovesick, the lonely; those who make mistakes in public, those who apologize, the silent, the talkative?

Do you approve of torture under any circumstances? Which?

What form of torture do you favor — physical, psychological, etc.?

Do you approve or disapprove of euthanasia? For others?
For yourself?

What form of euthanasia do you prefer? For others? For yourself? Is cost an issue? Would you prefer that your death be carried out by someone other than yourself? Close friends? Family members? If a doctor shows up bearing a lethal injection, would you feel it improper to refuse?

Which bodily functions do you find the most embarrassing to discuss?

Are there things you would say to one sex but not to the other?

The Uniform

Of the sleeves, I remember their weight, like wet wool,
on my arms, and the empty ends which hung past my hands.
Of the body of the shirt, I remember the large buttons
and larger buttonholes, which made a rack of wheels
down my chest and could not be quickly unbuttoned.
Of the collar, I remember its thickness without starch,
by which it lay against my clavicle without moving.
Of my trousers, the same — heavy, bulky, slow to give
for a leg, a crowded feeling, a molasses to walk in.
Of my boots, I remember the brittle soles, of a material
that had not been made love to by any natural substance,
and the laces: ropes to make prisoners of my feet.
Of the helmet, I remember the webbed, inner liner,
a brittle plastic underwear on which wobbled
the crushing steel pot then strapped at the chin.
Of the mortar, I remember the mortar plate,
heavy enough to kill by weight, which I carried by rope.
Of the machine gun, I remember the way it fit
behind my head and across my shoulder blades
as I carried it, or, to be precise, as it rode me.
Of tactics, I remember the likelihood of shooting
the wrong man, the weight of the rifle bolt, the difficulty
of loading while prone, the shock of noise.
For earplugs, some used cigarette filters or toilet paper.
I don't hear well now, for a man of my age,
and the doctor says my ears were damaged and asks
if I was in the Army, and of course I was but then
a wounded eardrum wasn't much in the scheme.

Ending with a Line from Lear

I will try to remember. It was light.
It was also dark, in the grave. I could feel
how dark it was, how black it would be
without my father. When he was gone.
But he was not gone, not yet. He was only
a corpse, and I could still touch him
that afternoon. Earlier the same afternoon.
This is the one thing that scares me:
losing my father. I don't want him to go.
I am a young man. I will never be older.
I am wearing a tie and a watch. The sky,
gray, hangs over everything. Today
the sky has no curve to it, and no end.
He is deep into his mission. He has business
to attend to. He wears a tie but no watch.
I will skip a lot of what happens next.
Then the moment comes. Everything, everything
has been said, and the wheels start to turn.
They roll, the straps unwind, and the coffin
begins to descend. Into the awful damp.
Into the black center of the earth. I
am being left behind. The center of my body
sinks down into the cold fire of the grave.
But still my feet stand on top of the dirt.
My father's grave. I will never again.
Never. Never. Never. Never. Never.

The Book of the Dead Man

1994

Live as if you were already dead.

ZEN ADMONITION

The Book of the Dead Man (#1)

1. About the Dead Man

The dead man thinks he is alive when he sees blood in his stool.
Seeing blood in his stool, the dead man thinks he is alive.
He thinks himself alive because he has no future.
Isn't that the way it always was, the way of life?
Now, as in life, he can call to people who will not answer.
Life looks like a white desert, a blaze of today in which nothing
        distinct can be made out, seen.
To the dead man, guilt and fear are indistinguishable.
The dead man cannot make out the spider at the center of its web.
He cannot see the eyelets in his shoes and so wears them unlaced.
He reads the large type and skips the fine print.
His vision surrounds a single tree, lost as he is in a forest.
From his porcelain living quarters, he looks out at a fiery plain.
His face is pressed against a frameless window.
Unable to look inside, unwilling to look outside, the man who is
        dead is like a useless gift in its box waiting.
It will have its yearly anniversary, but it would be wrong to call it
        a holiday.

2. More About the Dead Man

The dead man can balance a glass of water on his head without
        trembling.
He awaits the autopsy on the body discovered on the beach beneath
        the cliff.
Whatever passes through the dead man's mouth is expressed.
Everything that enters his mouth comes out of it.
He is willing to be diagnosed, as long as it won't disturb his future.
Stretched out, he snaps back like elastic.
Rolled over, he is still right-side-up.
When there is no good or bad, no useful or useless, no up, no down,
        no right way, no perfection, then okay it's not necessary
        that there be direction: up is down.
The dead man has the rest of his life to wait for color.
He finally has a bird's-eye view of the white hot sun.
He finally has a complete sentence, from his head to his feet.
He is, say, America, but he will soon be, say, Europe.
It will be necessary merely to cross the ocean and pop up in the new
        land, and the dead man doesn't need to swim.
It's the next best thing to talking to people in person.

The Book of the Dead Man (#3)

1. About the Beginnings of the Dead Man

When the dead man throws up, he thinks he sees his inner life.

Seeing his vomit, he thinks he sees his inner life.

Now he can pick himself apart, weigh the ingredients, research
his makeup.

He wants to study things outside himself if he can find them.

Moving, the dead man makes the sound of bone on bone.

He bends a knee that doesn't wish to bend, he raises an arm that
argues with a shoulder, he turns his head by throwing it
wildly to the side.

He envies the lobster the protective sleeves of its limbs.

He believes the jellyfish has it easy, floating, letting everything pass
through it.

He would like to be a starfish, admired for its shape long after.

Everything the dead man said, he now takes back.

Not as a lively young man demonstrates sincerity or regret.

A young dead man and an old dead man are two different things.

A young dead man is oil, an old dead man is water.

A young dead man is bread and butter, an old dead man is bread and
water — it's a difference in construction, also architecture.

The dead man was there in the beginning: to the dead man, the sky
is a crucible.

In the dead man's lifetime, the planet has changed from lava to ash
to cement.

But the dead man flops his feathers, he brings his wings up over
his head and has them touch, he bends over with his beak
to the floor, he folds and unfolds at the line where his
armor creases.

The dead man is open to change and has deep pockets.

The dead man is the only one who will live forever.

2. More About the Beginnings of the Dead Man

One day the dead man looked up into the crucible and saw the sun.
The dead man in those days held the sky like a small globe, like a
      patchwork ball, like an ultramarine bowl.
The dead man softened it, kneaded it, turned it and gave it volume.
He thrust a hand deep into it and shaped it from the inside out.
He blew into it and pulled it and stretched it until it became full-
      sized, a work of art created by a dead man.
The excellence of it, the quality, its character, its fundamental
      nature, its raison d'être, its "it" were all indebted to the
      dead man.

The dead man is the flywheel of the spinning planet.
The dead man thinks he can keep things the same by not moving.
By not moving, the dead man maintains the status quo at the center
      of change.
The dead man, by not moving, is an explorer: he follows his nose.
When it's not personal, not profound, he can make a new
      world anytime.
The dead man is the future, was always the future, can never be
      the past.
Like God, the dead man existed before the beginning, a time marked
      by galactic static.
Now nothing remains of the first static that isn't music, fashioned
      into melody by the accidents of interval.
Now nothing more remains of silence that isn't sound.
The dead man has both feet in the past and his head in the clouds.

The Book of the Dead Man (#6)

1. About the Dead Man's Speech

Will the dead man speak? Speak, says the lion, and the dead man
        makes the sound of a paw in the dirt.
When the dead man paws the dirt, lions feel the trembling of
        the pride.
Speak, says the tree, and the dead man makes the sound of tree
        bark enlarging its circumference, a slight inhalation.
Speak, says the wind, and the dead man exhales all at once.
Whoever told the dead man to be quiet was whistling in the dark.
To the dead man, the dark is all words as white is all colors.
The dead man obliges, he cooperates, he speaks when spoken to, so
        when the dirt says Speak, he says what erosion says.
And when the air says Speak, the dead man says what a cavity says.
The dead man knows the syntax of rivers and rocks, the one a
        long ever-qualifying sentence for which no last words
        suffice, the other the briefest and most steadfast exercise
        in exclusion.
The dead man is a rock carried by a river, a pebble borne by air, a
        sound carved into frequencies infrequently registered.

2. More About the Dead Man's Speech

The dead man is part of the chorus that sings the music of
        the spheres.

Dead man's music uses the harmonics and parasitics of sound, in
        bands of low frequencies caught in ground waves that hug
        the terrain as they go, and in ultrahigh megacycles that
        dent the ionosphere and refract over the horizon.

The dead man makes no distinction between the music he hears and
        the music he only knows about.

There are five elements in the dead man's music (time, tempo, key,
        harmony and counterpoint) and two factors (silence
        and chance).

To the dead man, the wrinkled back of a hand is a score to be read.

The balding top and back of his head are a kind of braille awaiting a
        blind conductor.

The dead man's bone-sounds and teeth-clacks are a form of
        tuning up.

Sad music brings artificial tears to the dead man's dilated eyes.

All things being equal, the dead man is not fussy about pitch
        and dissonance.

His inner ear is set to hear euphonic consonants.

The dead man sings in the shower, in good weather and bad,
        without knowing a song.

He hums the tunes of commercials without the words, sympathetic
        vibrations.

He has ideas for musical instruments made of roots and feathers,
        harps that use loose dirt something like an interrupted
        hourglass.

When the dead man, in a gravelly voice, sings gospel, hammers
        descend upon anvils.

The Book of the Dead Man (#11)

1. About the Dead Man and Medusa

When the dead man splays his arms and legs, he is a kind of Medusa.

Thinking himself Medusa, the dead man further splays his arms
and legs.

Now he can shake it, toss it, now he can weave a seductive glamour
into the source of all feelings, a glamour known to roots
and to certain eyeless vermin of interiors.

The dead man knows the power of hair by its absence, hairy as
he was at the near edge of immortality while his fame
kept growing.

The dead man uses the ingredients of cosmetic products made just
for men.

He pares his nails in the background, just as Joyce, the elder
statesman of rainy statelessness, pictured the alienated
artist after work.

He snips the little hairs from his nose and from inside the shells
of his ears, for the artist must be laid bare in a light
easily diverted.

He wears the guarded fashions of loose clothing so that changes
that might offend — the loss of a limb or a sudden hollow
in the chest — may go undetected.

Mortal among immortals, the dead man can change you to stone.

2. More About the Dead Man and Medusa

The dead man mistakes his rounded shoulders for wings.
His shoulder blades suggesting wings, the dead man steals a
        peripheral glance and shrugs, causing a breeze.
While the dead man's nails keep growing, the dead man has claws.
Once the dead man has lain in the earth long enough, he will have
        snakes for hair.
Who could have guessed that the dead man was this much of
        a woman?
Who knows better the extraneous ripple of a long yawn?
In the theory of the dead man, nothing accounts for his maternity.
The dead man will not move out of harm's way, nor leave his
        children, he repeatedly gives his life for them.
Who else may someday be beheaded by a sword made out of water
        and weed?
Mortal among immortals, the dead man strangles the moon
        in saliva.
Domed and tentacled, capped and limbed, the dead man resembles
        a jellyfish.
Under his wig, the dead man's waxed skull belies the soft spot on a
        baby's head that turns whosoever knows of it to mush.
The dead man speaks also for those who were turned into stone.

The Book of the Dead Man (#13)

1. About the Dead Man and Thunder

When the dead man hears thunder, he thinks someone is speaking.
Hearing the thunder, the dead man thinks he is being addressed.
He thinks he is being addressed because the sound contains heat and
        humidity — or groaning and salivation.
Isn't that always the way with passionate language — heat and
        humidity?
The dead man passes burning bushes and parting seas without inner
        trembling, nor does he smear his door with blood.
The dead man can only be rattled physically, never emotionally.
The dead man's neuroses cancel one another out like a floor of snakes.
He is the Zen of open doors, he exists in the zone of the selfless, he
        has visions and an ear for unusual music.
Now he can hear the swirling of blood beneath his heartbeat.
Now he can fall in love with leaves — with the looping lift and fall
        of love.
Naturally, the dead man is receptive, has his antennas out, perches
        on the edge of sensitivity to receive the most wanton
        prayer and the least orderly of wishes.
To the dead man, scared prayer isn't worth a damn.
The dead man erases the word for God to better understand divinity.
When nothing interferes, nothing interrupts, nothing sustains or
        concludes, then there's no need to separate doing from
        not-doing or to distribute the frequencies of the thunder
        into cause and effect.
The dead man speaks God's language.

2. More About the Dead Man and Thunder

The dead man counts the seconds between lightning and thunder to
       see how far he is from God.
The dead man counts God among his confidants: they whisper.
The dead man hears the screams of roots being nibbled by rodents.
He notes the yelps of pebbles forced to maneuver and of boulders
       pinned into submission.
He feels the frustration of bodily organs forced to be quiet.
He thinks it's no wonder the sky cries and growls when it can.
The dead man's words can be just consonants, they can be only
       vowels, they can pile up behind his teeth like sagebrush on
       a fence or float like paper ashes to the top of fathomless
       corridors, they can echo like wind inside a skull or flee
       captivity like balloons that have met a nail.
The dead man serves an indeterminate sentence in an elastic cell.
He hears a voice in the thunder and sees a face in the lightning, and
       there's a smell of solder at the junction of earth and sky.

The Book of the Dead Man (#14)

1. About the Dead Man and Government

Under Communism, the dead man's poems were passed around
hand-to-hand.

The dead man's poems were dog-eared, positively, under
Communism.

The dead man remembers Stalin finally strangling on verbs.

And the dead man's poems were mildewed from being hidden in
basements under Fascism.

Embedded in the dead man is a picture of Mussolini hanging from
a noun.

The dead man didn't know what to say first, after the oppression
was lifted.

The green cast of mildew gave way to the brown stain of coffee
upon coffee.

Suddenly, a pen was a pen and an alligator only an alligator.

A pig in boots was no longer a human being, a dead man was no
longer alive though everyone knew better.

Now the dead man feels the steamy weight of the world.

He trembles at the press of the witch hunters, their clothes
like night.

He has in his memory all tortures, genocides, trials and lockups.

He sees the lovers of pressed flowers brought down by botanical
poverty.

He sees the moviegoers, who kissed through the credits, stunned
by the sudden light after the ending.

In the lobby, the dead man's manuscripts went under coats and
into pockets.

Then they all went off to spill coffee and argue ethics.

The dead man is the anarchist whose eyes look up through the
bottom of the glass raised in toast.

The dead man is sweeter than life. Sweeter than life is the life of the
dead man.

2. More About the Dead Man and Government

The dead man votes once for Abraham Lincoln, but that's it.
That's all he's time for (one man/one vote), so the dead man votes
        for Abe Lincoln.
The dead man votes with his feet, lashing his possessions to his back
        as if he were Ulysses tied to the mast to resist the siren call
        to stay put.
The dead man votes with a gun, disassembling it, beating the parts
        into scrap metal for farm implements.
The dead man votes with wet hands, a fishy smell lemon juice
        can't cut.
He comes in off the boat, off the farm, from the cash register
        and the time clock to throw down a ballot.
The dead man is there when the revolution stalls in a pile of
        young corpses.
It is the dead man's doing when the final tally is zero to zero.
The dead man is the freight man on the swing shift at the end
        of the line.
The dead man remembers the railroads run down by automobiles,
        the fields commandeered for storm sewers, the
        neighborhoods knifed by highways.
The dead man thinks a dead Lincoln is still better than the
        other candidates.
He knows that death stops nothing, and he hopes to be placed
        among the censored.
His immortality depends on the quality of his enemies.
He sees a wormy democracy spilling from the graveyards, its fists
        flailing at the target.
There is hope, there is still hope, there is always hope.
The dead man and his fellow dead are the buried treasure which will
        ransom the future.
You have only to believe in the past.

The Book of the Dead Man (#15)

1. About the Dead Man and Rigor Mortis

The dead man thinks his resolve has stiffened when the
      ground dries.
Feeling the upward flow of moisture, the dead man thinks his
      resolve has stiffened.
The dead man's will, will be done.
The dead man's backbone stretches from rung to rung, from here to
      tomorrow, from a fabricated twinge to virtual agony.
The dead man's disks along his spine are like stepping-stones across
      a lake, the doctor told him "jelly doughnuts" when they
      ruptured, this is better.
The dead man's hernial groin is like a canvas bridge across a
      chasm, the doctor said "balloon" when they operated,
      this is better.
The dead man's toes are like sanded free forms and his heels are as
      smooth as the backs of new shoes, the doctor said "corns"
      when they ached, this is better.
The dead man's eyes are like tiny globes in water, continental
      geographies in microcosm, all the canyons are visible, now
      washed of random hairs that rooted, now free of the
      strangulated optics of retinal sense, this is better.
All the dead man's organs, his skin, muscles, tendons, arteries, veins,
      valves, networks, relays — the whole shebang hums like a
      quickly deserted hardware store.
To the dead man, a head of cabbage is a forerunner of nutrients.
The dead man's garden foreshadows the day it is to be plowed under,
      agriculture being one of the ancient Roman methods for
      burying the Classics, the other was war.
No one can argue with the dead man, he brooks no interference
      between the lightning and ground, his determination
      is legendary.

2. More About the Dead Man and Rigor Mortis

You think it's funny, the dead man being stiff?
You think it's an anatomically correct sexual joke?
You think it's easy, being petrified?
You think it's just one of those things, being turned to stone?
Who do you think turns the dead man to stone anyway?
Who do you think got the idea first?
You think it's got a future, this being dead?
You think it's in the cards, you think the thunder spoke?
You think he thought he was dead, or thought he fancied he was
       dead, or imagined he could think himself dead, or really
       knew he was dead?
You think he knew he knew?
You think it was predetermined?
You think when he stepped out of character he was different?
What the hell, what do you think?
You think it's funny, the way the dead man is like lightning, going
       straight into the ground?
You think it's hilarious, comedy upstanding, crackers to make
       sense of?

The Book of the Dead Man (#19)

1. About the Dead Man and Winter

When the dead man's skin turns black and blue, he thinks it
 is winter.
In winter, the dead man gathers and insists, slipping his collective
 unconscious forward like a blue glacier.
When flowers turn under, he sees the stars blooming above, florid in
 their icy reaches.
When leaves desert the trees, he reads the calligraphy of the limbs.
The dead man endures material eternity with a shy smile.
The dead man in winter envelops, he encircles, he reaches around
 him like the possibility of wings on a butterfly.
In winter, the dead man tries on chaos in its fixed form.
His hollow deformity lasts and lasts, his shapely presence maintains
 the look it was given: that much longer is he gripped.
The dead man knows why the cherry tree waits for spring.
The dead man senses the earth going to sleep, he feels the vast
 organism within which he is a brainy parasite sputter
 and collapse.
The dead man waits with the bear in its cave and the rabbit in its
 hutch in the snow.
To reduce pain and swelling, the dead man takes six months
 of winter.
The dead man swallows winter, he applies it, he rubs it in, he wears
 it for support.
The dead man's head in winter lies like a cabbage in repose.
Under a blanket of dormant weeds, he basks in the brittle formality
 of the gray salon.
When there is no adversity, no rise and fall, no ascension, no decline,
 no frost too early, no season too soon, then there's no
 planet too unstable, no ship in the sky better than another
 for the journey of a lifetime.
The dead man's white flame is the last trace of ash.

The dead man through the scrawny stalks of beheaded weeds offers
　　up the slightest scent of a place where live fish wait to be
　　thawed and roots fall silent.
No one knows better than the dead man the chalk made from
　　common materials that accretes around each organism
　　deprived of water.
The dead man in winter is not just winter.

2. More About the Dead Man and Winter

The dead man in winter is the source of spring.
The dead man turns equally to all seasons with the cachet of a guest
　　only momentarily served and all too soon departed.
What do you mean, not wiping the glass of the dead man's
　　fingerprints?
What do you mean, disengaging from his small talk to rush to the
　　side of fake heads of state?
The dead man freezes out the relentlessly glamorous, he does not
　　welcome the vain nor host the proud, he turns from
　　photos with too much hair and tilted heads, he absconds
　　before the heat goes on in the bedroom.
To the dead man, all social gatherings are wintry.
To the dead man, a turn of the head leads to an ear full of dirt.
O winter, the season of warm hors d'oeuvres and cold counsel.
The dead man is the drumbeat of winter.
Among the frozen, among the polar thinking caps and arctic
　　questions, among the sled tracks and boot crevasses,
　　among every poised paw print and running hoof mark,
　　among the etched signatures of survival that everywhere
　　mark the surface, the dead man models for eternity.
The dead man in winter is in heaven.

The Book of the Dead Man (#21)

1. About the Dead Man's Happiness

When the dead man hears the thunderous steps of an ant, he
         feels eager.
Sensing the reaching of a root, the dead man swells with metabolic
         anticipation.
The dead man loves the snoring of the sea and the absentminded
         whistling of the wind.
He doesn't need much if it will rain now and then so that the weeds
         can flourish and a simple buttercup can get in position to
         sully a nose.
He likes listening to an ear of corn.
He loves the feeling of the wood when he drums his fingers.
He grows giddy at the thought of elk contesting and wolves
         patrolling.
The dead man does not choose sides between fact and fiction,
         night and day, beauty and truth, youth and age, or men
         and women.
The dead man can spend fifteen minutes opening and closing an
         umbrella, what a contraption!, its cone changes to a
         triangle and then a parabola, reordering geometry.
The dead man has turned his back on the planed edge of memory,
         each face from the past now bears the freshness of a
         cut orange.
The dead man's blood can be brought to a boil by a kiss, but also
         by dumb remarks about cows.
The dead man is an outsider by choice, unwilling to give up even
         so much as the graphite dunce cap of a wooden pencil
         and how it feels.
The dead man is one example, the rest to be filled in.
The dead man has it all, even the worms and the dogs.

2. More About the Dead Man's Happiness

The dead man wanted more until he had everything and wanted
        none of it.
At nerve's end, the dead man felt frayed and scattered: the profit
        takers wanted their share, and the bloodletters, the
        parasites, the actual doctors, the patient embalmers, the
        donors, the grocers, the tailors, the candy makers, and
        himself, too, lunging.
One day the dead man decided to keep himself as he was —
        saw-toothed, tilted, uneven.
The dead man decided to stay short, lose his hair, wear glasses, get
        heartburn, be pained, and thrill to his ignorance.
To the dead man, more mystery means more.
More fog, more vapors, more darkness, more distance, more time,
        more absence — to the dead man, all is everything.
Put it down to the dead man's love of the watery rays of starlight.
Put it down to the dead man's lamentations.
One day something in the dead man rose from his body with a creak.
Under blank retinal covers he felt himself fill with happiness.
When he saw that he had displaced his weight in water, Archimedes
        cried, "Eureka!"
The dead man did the same with substance and shadow.

The Book of the Dead Man (#23)

1. About the Dead Man and His Masks

When the dead man thinks himself exposed, he puts on a mask.

Thinking himself exposed, the dead man puts on a mask.

Before he needed a mask, he wore his medals on his chest and his
      heart on his sleeve.

The dead man wears the mask of tomfoolery, the mask of
      assimilation, the mask of erasure, the scarred mask, the
      teen mask, the mask with the built-in *oh,* the laughing
      mask, the crying mask, the secretive mask, the telltale
      mask, and of course the death mask.

The dead man's masks are as multifarious as the wiles of a spider left
      to work in the bushes.

To the dead man, a spider's web is also a mask, and he wears it.

The trail of a slug is a mask, and the vapors from underground fires
      are a mask, and the dead light of sunset is a mask, and the
      dead man wears each of them.

The dead man curtained off the world, now everything between
      them is a mask.

He weaves masks of sand and smoke, of refracted light and
      empty water.

The dead man takes what the world discards: hair and bones, urine
      and blood, ashes and sewage.

The dead man, reconstituted, will not stay buried, reappearing in
      disguises that fool no one yet cast doubt.

He comes to the party wearing the face of this one or that one,
      scattering the shadows as he enters.

When there is no one face, no two faces, no fragility of disposition,
      no anticipation, no revelation at midnight, then naturally
      years pass without anyone guessing the identity of the
      dead man.

It is no longer known if the dead man was at the funeral.

2. More About the Dead Man and His Masks

The dead man's mask prefigures all isms such as surrealism,
        patriotism, cronyism, futurism, Darwinism, barbarism,
        dadaism, Catholicism, Judaism, etc.

Many of the dead man's masks are museum pieces: final expressions
        from death row, those startled at the last second in
        Pompeii or Dresden or Hiroshima, faces surprised in the
        trenches, the terror of furnaces and lime, a look formed
        from suffocation or lengthy bleeding or embalming.

The dead man apologizes for leaving a sewing machine and an
        umbrella on the operating table.

The dead man catalogs war memorials, potter's fields, he takes
        stock of undiscovered suicides, pseudonyms and all
        instances of anonymity.

The dead man's masks are composed of incongruous materials
        accidentally combined and are as rare and wild as certain
        edible fungi that closely resemble poisonous mushrooms.

He doffs his hat to long hair, moustaches and beards, but does not
        give himself away.

He greets the grieving, the relieved, the startled, the victimized and
        the triumphant without letting on.

The dead man's hands are twice as expressive in gloves, his feet
        deprived of their arches gain momentum in shoes, and his
        mask shields him from those who wish to trade
        knowledge for truth.

The dead man's first mask was a hand over his mouth.

The Book of the Dead Man (#29)

1. About the Dead Man and Sex

The dead man lowers standards, ha ha, sinking, steadily sinking.
The dead man is jovial ha in the tide pool peaceful zzz among the
        tubers thoughtful uh uh in the basement ho ho creating
        humph humph the foundations of modern thought.
The dead man throws fuel on the fire.
The dead man throws in spoonerisms, being lone bonely, he gathers
        the wordless words, the articulation of knee jerks and
        other reflexive gestures, the spill of an orgasm.
He puts in the *whoosh,* the *ssss,* the *ahhh* and *oh oh oh.*
He is hot for the body, heaping moan on moan.
The dead man is the outcome of ecstasy, everyone knows it and
        wants more.
The dead man's lapidary but orgasmic, nothing new there.
The dead man is the depository of fixed form, the vault for a cool
        customer, safe harbor, still he loves the juiced-up joining
        in the midst of love.
The dead man lets the clock expire to be there.
He is a sponge that never dries, absorbing the dark water.
Omigoodness, the dead man does things.

2. More About the Dead Man and Sex

The dead man speaks the lingo of sizzle, the grammar of quickened
        breathing, he states the obvious: more is more.
To the dead man, the new moon is a rounded promise of romance.
The dead man's wounded moon heals over each attempt to explore
        her and comes again to flirt in the dark.
The dead man's understanding of the moon goes well beyond
        her face.
It travels beyond her light side, reaching around blindly but
        with faith.
The dead man seeks the becalmed, the held, the immobilized in
        himself and sets it free.
Therefore the dead man studies the day sky to see the early moon.
He knows the moon is the better half of himself, that he is
        incomplete without her, and he cradles her on his
        brow as she rises.
All these things the dead man does and more.

The Book of the Dead Man (#30)

1. About the Dead Man's Late Nights

When the dead man cannot go to sleep, he squeezes blood from
      a stone.

Remember, the dead man is lapidary but orgasmic.

The dead man extracts blood, bile, semen, saliva, hair and teeth.

He weighs fillings and counts moles.

He takes a look at himself in two mirrors at once.

Front to back, side to side, top to bottom, the dead man is a matrix
      of handprints, stitches, whiskers, tiny volcanoes where
      vaccinations took, mineral deposits left to unclaimed
      salvage, congealed oil of an insufficient tolerance, wax
      and water.

There are many ways to look at the dead man but only one way to
      understand him.

The dead man can pass through a keyhole, the lens of an eye, the eye
      of a needle, walls that have neither doors nor windows.

He can disappear and reappear, he can summon feelings, he can get
      down on his knees, he can wave from afar, he can tie
      himself in knots, he can twist a thought or turn it over, he
      can count sheep, but sometimes he cannot go to sleep.

What then does he say when it's why not?

He says absolutely nothing, precisely nothing, eloquently nothing.

The dead man has dissolved the knot in which his tongue was tied.

Whereas formerly the dead man was sometimes beside himself, now
      he is one.

Whereas formerly the dead man cohered in the usual way, now he
      thinks dissolution is good for the soul, a form of
      sacramental undoing viewed through a prism, a kind of
      philosophic nakedness descending a staircase.

He wants to be awake at the very end.

So the dead man gets up at night to walk on glass.

He tumbles out of his sheets to consort with worms.

He holds back the hands of the clock, he squeezes the light in his
    fists, he runs in place like a man on a treadmill who has
    asked a doctor to tell him what to do.

2. More About the Dead Man's Late Nights

The dead man mistakes numbness for sleep.
He mistakes frostbite for the tingle of anticipation, a chill for fresh
    air, fever for lust.
He thinks he could throw a stone to kingdom come, but he is wrong.
He is used to being taken for granite, for a forehead of stars or a
    swath of matted grass.
But the dead man is more than the rivulets chiseled into the marker.
He is far more than the peaceful view at the downhill border, the
    floral entry, the serenity.
The dead man is the transparent reed that made music from
    thin air.
His life has been a die-hard joy beyond the sweep of starlight, he
    transcends the black hole, he has weight and specific
    gravity, he reflects, he is rained on.
The dead man does not live in a vacuum, he swallows air and its
    ill effects.
The dead man is rapt to stay the course, fervent for each spoke of
    the sun.
The dead man is mad to ride the wheel to the end of the circle.

Ardor: The Book of the Dead Man, Vol. 2

1997

*For a long time pure linear painting drove me mad until I met van Gogh,
who painted neither lines nor shapes but inert things in nature as if they
were having convulsions.*

ARTAUD: "VAN GOGH: THE MAN SUICIDED BY SOCIETY"

To be at all — what is better than that?

WALT WHITMAN

The Book of the Dead Man (#34)

1. About the Dead Man, Ashes and Dust

The dead man is slag ash soot cinders grime powder embers flakes
     chips slivers snippets lava and sand.
He is fumes fog smoke and vapor.
Do not mistake the exhausted dead man for the mangled, dissolved
     or atomized.
His mark is not a blemish on the earth but a rising tide of
     consciousness.
His tracks are not the footprints in the foyer but thoughts brought
     to bear.
The letter of the dead man impedes, but the letter and the spirit of
     the dead man together animate.
The dead man is not the end but the beginning.
To conceive of the dead man is the first act of birth, incipient.
The dead man was first.
At the table, nothing more can be poured into his empty bowl.
His is the whisper that cannot be traced, the hollow that cannot
     be leveled, the absolute, the groundless ideal, the pure —
     in all respects, the substance of the honorific.
That is, everything outside the dead man is now inside the
     dead man.

2. More About the Dead Man, Ashes and Dust

The dead man, Ladies and Gentlemen, clears his throat.
He adopts the rhetorical posture of one to whom things happen.
He rises, he appears, he seems to be, he is.
It is the dead man's turn to toast the living, his role to oversee the
       merriment, his part to invoke the spirits and calculate
       the dusk.
He is recondite in the dun evenings, deep in the sallow dawn, fit
       for contemplation all day, he is able to sit still, he lets
       his dreams simmer in the milky overcast of a day
       commonly pictured.
Who but the dead man has better drawn the covers over his head?
What better could the dead man have done to show his good will
       than to keep his secrets buried?
No one hath done as much.
Consider where the dead man goes at the end of the day.
Picture his brusque exits, reconsider his gruff respects, listen to
       his last words that found the nearest ear.
When the dead man clears his throat, it may be first words or
       last words.
When there is no birthday, no anniversary, no jubilee, no spree, no
       holiday, no one mass, meeting or service, then naturally it
       is up to each person whether to go ahead or turn back.
The dead man is 360 degrees of reasoning, three sides of a syllogism
       and four sides of a simple box.

The Book of the Dead Man (#35)

1. About the Dead Man and Childhood

In an evening of icicles, tree branches crackling as they break frozen
       sap, a gull's bark shattering on snow, the furnace turned
       down for the night, the corpse air without exits — here the
       dead man reenters his fever.

The paste held, that was dry and brittle.

The rotting rubber band stuck to the pack of playing cards to keep
       it together.

In the boy's room, the balsa balanced where there had once
       been glue.

Recognition kept its forms in and out of season.

Why not, then, this sweaty night of pursuit?

He has all of himself at his disposal.

He has every musical note, every word, though certain notes of the
       piano have evaporated.

Shall he hear them anyway?

The dead man's boyhood home withholds from its current
       occupants the meaning of desecration, nor shall they be
       the destroyers of the past in their own minds.

You too have seen anew the giant rooms of the little house in which
       you were a child.

You have seen the so-heavy door that now barely resists a light hand.

You have walked down the once endless corridors that now end
       abruptly.

Were you so small then that now you are in the way?

You too sat at the impossibly high kitchen table with your feet
       dangling, drawn down by the heavy shoes.

All this and more the dead man remembers the connective quality of.

In those days, there was neither here nor now, only there and the
       time it would take to reach it.

2. More About the Dead Man and Childhood

After Adam ate the apple, there was one more, and then one more...
After Orpheus looked back, there was another and another...
The dead man discerns betwixt and between, he knows mania
      and depression, he has within him the two that make
      one, the opposites that attract, the summer pain and
      the winter pain.
He walks both the road of excess and the least path, and lives most
      in the slow-to-ripen spring and extended autumn.
The dead man does not come when called but tries to hit a baseball
      in the dusk.
He does not yet know he wants to ride the horse that took the bit in
      its mouth.
He lives in the attic and the big closet where the radio parts and the
      extra glassware hold their codes.
He is the initiate.
He feigns nothing, he has nothing else in mind, later he will be
      charged with having been a boy.
Even now, in May and September he feels the throbbing tissue of
      that fallow world from which he was forced to be free.
The dead man in adulthood knows the other side, and he winces at
      the fragility of the old songbooks, taped and yellowed,
      held there in time.

The Book of the Dead Man (#42)

1. About the Dead Man's Not Telling

The dead man encounters horrific conditions infused with beauty.
He looks and sees, dare you see with his unblinkered eyes.
He sniffs and ingests, dare you do the same as he.
He hears and feels, dare you secure such stimuli and endure
      the heart.
He sets foot on the anomalies, he traverses the interior laden with
      the screams of witnesses underfoot.
He walks among the pines crackling with the soon-to-be-broken
      backs of new life.
He freely rests among the appetites of the unsatisfied.
He bites off the head of the Buddha.
The dead man has seen bad Buddhahood.
He has doubled back, he has come around, he has cut across, he has
      taken the long shortcut.
What is out there, that germinates?
The dead man knows that there is no luck but dumb luck, no heart
      that will not skip, no pulse that does not race.
Things go, time goes, while the dead man stays.

2. More About the Dead Man's Not Telling

Has not the dead man asked a basic question?

Did he not lie in the crib like a question mark without a sentence?

Did he not encode the vitality of roots, the beauty of leaves, the
        kinetics of branches, the rapture of the sun, the solace of
        the moon, even the hollow that shapes the seed?

The dead man is the one to ask when there is asking.

Those who invest in the past or future shall forfeit the dead man's
        objectivity, his elasticity strung from down-and-dirty to
        up-and-ready.

When the oracle spoke, the dead man listened like a shell.

When the quixotic signaled from the wood, the dead man grasped
        the new life that needed no more plasma than the dew.

How comely the horrific consequences, how amiable the gorgeous
        advantage of the newly born.

Things go, time goes, but the dead man goes nowhere without you.

You who told him know what is on the dead man's mind.

You at the fringe, the margin, the edge, the border, the outpost, the
        periphery, the hinterland, you at the extremity, you at the
        last, counterpoised, have caught the inference.

The dead man counts by ones and is shy before your mildest
        adoration.

The Book of the Dead Man (#43)

1. About the Dead Man and Desire

When the dead man itches, he thinks he has picked up a splinter.

Unable to free himself of an itch, the dead man thinks he has
        a splinter.

The dead man looks at a praying mantis and sees a pair of tweezers.

He offers himself to be walked on by claws.

He waits for the odd fox to trot across his chest and strings of ants to
        scrape him pore to pore.

He anticipates the flaying action of chemicals and the sponge baths
        of the rain.

The dead man, scoured, is the ruby servant of the vineyard.

The dead man is the salt of the earth, the dust and the sawdust, the
        honey in the wine.

Hence, his thoughts must rise to the moon and beyond to take his
        mind from that splinter if it is a splinter, that itch if an
        itch is what it is.

Everything the dead man thinks has its other side.

The dead man thinks Saturn has been much married but
        forever lonely.

2. More About the Dead Man and Desire

If he were just valves and glue, just honey and chocolate, just hot and
        cold, the dead man's thoughts would not hop, skip and
        jump so.

If he were just comparative, if he were absolute, if he knew his own
        mind, the dead man's heart would not race so.

Who but the dead man wonders which of its moons Jupiter favors?

Who knows better than the dead man in his bones the pitch at
        which the earth breathes?

The dead man is rapt before the altar of consciousness.

He enters the forbidden realms of experience without penalty.

To the dead man, there is something grave about umbrellas,
        something sinister about servitude, something
        debilitating about knowledge — like sunlight on slugs.

The dead man rolls back into place the rock that was moved to
        find out.

Like Sisyphus, the dead man wants what he has.

When there is no more meek, no vainglorious, no catch-as-catch-
        can, no inheritance, no opportunity knocking that is not
        also the wind, then naturally the dead man lives for love.

The dead man, fervent to feel, makes no distinction between a
        splinter and a stinger that cost something its life.

The Book of the Dead Man (#47)

1. Toaster, Kettle and Breadboard

The dead man lives in the flesh, in memory, in absentia, in fact and
    fiction, by chance and by nature.
What are we to make of his continuous use of everyday objects?
For the dead man's fingerprints are everywhere: his crumbs, his
    residue, the marks his tools made.
The dead man corks and uncorks the passable wine.
He needles the bad meat to make it tender, he breads the wings of
    the chicken, he takes from the incendiary oven his meal
    at leisure.
The dead man has no stomach for ordinary indigestion.

2. More About the Dead Man's Toaster, Kettle and Breadboard

The dead man sees fireweed grow from scorched ground.
He sees the conspicuous consumption of Thoreau, the torch-
        bearing saviors of Walden.
He reckons up the passionate aesthetics devoid of the smell of ashes.
He notes the footprints on the rice paper of those who seek divine
        abstinence.
He records and distributes the knowledge of fair game.
Did the dead man eat roasted bread or drink from boiling water or
        take a piece of something, leaving the rest?
There is only the evidence of the dead man's estate.
There is only the proof of toaster, kettle and breadboard.
The dead man does not confuse plain water with weak tea or piety
        with indifference.
When there is no more appetite, no inhalation, no absorption, no
        osmosis, no digestion, then okay let the reverie commence
        in the ether.
The dead man lives in the meantime, the in-between time, the time it
        takes to boil, broil, bake and fry, assimilating the cooked
        and the raw, the beefy and the lean.
The dead man is himself an ample morsel-to-be, a tidbit, a
        sweetmeat, slices and scraps and a mouthful of quills.

The Book of the Dead Man (#54)

1. About the Dead Man and the Corpse of Yugoslavia

When the dead man feels nausea, he thinks he is in the Balkans.
Feeling nausea, the dead man thinks he is scattered body parts.
Dismemberment makes the dead man queasy — historically.
Is not the dead man a witness to every dole, lot and quota?
Was not the dead man in place when the Serbs shelled Sarajevo?
The dead man heard the shouts of the victims being pasted into
       history over brief captions.
He pointed a finger at the butcher Milosevic when the guns
       hammered the old city.
He shook his clenched fist at the genocide visited upon the Muslims,
       as it was and would be upon the churches, synagogues and
       mosques of the secessionary and independent.
He twisted and thrashed to transmit an underground murmur
       of conscience.
He gyrated, he spun, he literally threw himself into the air, he did
       everything possible to gain their attention but dance.
At a distance, the dead man's screams made a beautiful music.
Now the dead man, having lain down in flash fire and firestorm,
       bewitches his contemporaries.
The dead man proffers the scent of something left undone, but
       there are so few words for how a thing smells.
The dead man is the last one of many.

2. More About the Dead Man and the Corpse of Yugoslavia

The dead man sees the head, then the heart, of a dismembered State.

He sees the arms that tried to clap, the eyes that blinked and went
blank and were turned under.

He raises a fluttering flag held by the leg bone of the violated.

He hangs the dry tongues of the multitudes along the fences of
western Europe.

He mails the ears and lips to the West for overnight delivery.

The dead man is the inscriber of names and dates, the conveyor of
last wishes and words, secretary to a truce signed over the
scent of cremation.

When there is no more defense, no strategic withdrawal, no bargain,
no outcome, no resolution, then of course there's no
condemnation, no horror, no moral reality, nothing
intangible to impute dishonor to the victors.

The dead man is the spoils to which the victors pledge their
allegiance.

The dead man wonders why the hurry?

Meanwhile, the dead man certifies each eye extracted for an eye, each
tooth for a tooth: the whole carnivorous escapade.

The dead man picks among the living for future specimens.

The Book of the Dead Man (#58)

1. About the Dead Man Outside

They came to the door because he was small or went to some church
       or other or was seen in the company of girls or boys.
Well, he was small and went to synagogue and didn't know what to
       make of it.
They said he was from some tribe, but he didn't understand it.
They acted as if they knew what they were doing.
They were the executioners of brown eyes and brown hair, and he
       happened to have both.
Well, he said, and they went away before he awoke.
They were a dream he was having before he became the dead man.
Today the dead man lives where others died.
He passes the crematoriums without breathing.
He enters the pit graves and emerges ashen or lime-laced.
He shreds the beautiful tapestries of history and hangs in their place
       the rough shirts and dank pants forsaken at the showers,
       and the tiny work caps.
He mounts the hewn chips of shoesoles, the twisted spectacles, the
       tortured belts and suspenders, the stained handkerchiefs.
Here, he says, is history, maternity, inheritance.

2. More About the Dead Man Outside

Let none pardon the Devil lest he have to begin again.

Let no one weep easily, let no one build portfolios of disaster
        snapshots or record the lingo of the know-betters,
        let no one speak who has not considered the fatalities
        of geography.

The dead man does not suffer skinheads lightly, their evil is legion.

With an olive branch, he whips the villains into a frenzy of
        repentance.

The dead man tattoos the war criminals with the numbers.

The dead man wonders what America would be like if every war were
        a wall engraved with the names of the lost.

Well, they said, he was from some tribe or other, and he didn't
        understand it.

When the dead man was a dead child, he thought as a child.

Now the dead man lives that others may die, and dies that others
        may live.

Let the victims gather, the dead man stays on the outside looking in.

Let the saved celebrate, the dead man stands distant, remote.

The dead man listens for the sound of Fascist boots.

They will be going again to his grave to try to cut down his
        family tree.

This time the dead man will see them in hell.

The Book of the Dead Man (#62)

1. About the Dead Man Apart

When the dead man opens himself up, he is blown about,
	showered, shed, scattered, dismantled, diluted and
	diffused, not discarded.
When the dead man is unfolded — unbent and unbowed — he is
	gathered, consolidated and collected, not condensed.
The melee, the chaos, the disorder, the tumult — the dead man sleeps.
Libraries drift past laden with coffins of illusion.
Things truly dead lie buried in the commercial tide, sweep in on
	the sea.
The dead man is joyful in the future of his having said so.
What to do and where to be in the millennium is of the moment.
The dead man's old eyes peruse and otherwise overtake the
	intentions of blood on parchment, divinations and
	forecasts, the jubilee of a century of anticipation.
The dead man signs on and off, his silence is his assent.
His irretrievable warrant must live in the henceforth and the
	consequences.
His ardor shall endure, though it sag with the dew point.
The dead man too had fits of loneliness, from which he has
	recovered.
He sank to the depth of doubt and fell past time into vast confusion,
	from which he has recovered.
He slept with illusion and woke with unreality, from which he
	has recovered.
He made the mistake of youth, the error of age, the blunders, the
	bloopers, the false steps of left and right and of the
	deceptively wide middle way.
All the dead man wanted and wants, he has.
Where the sun has forgotten the moon, where the stars have
	forsaken the abyss and the very footing has moved on, the
	dead man knows his place.
The dead man is forever flagrant.

2. More About the Dead Man Apart

The dead man knows that death does not shine in the dark, as the
      wind is not blown about.
It is up to the dead man to subject himself to the subjective.
It is the dead man's fate to be passionately detached.
Who, facing the end, better hikes, hurries, treks and tours?
Who but the dead man, having all the time in the world, dispatches
      his intentions?
Go thou, says the dead man, thou book born in ignorance, go thou
      and do likewise, otherwise, elsewise, be not timid among
      the blind specialists.
The dead man does not pluck, cull or garner reality.
When there is no end result, no picaresque interval, no immediate or
      impending, nothing imminent that is not also the past,
      then why not roses and rubles, peace and prosperity, and
      okay it's not inconsequential to have come and gone.
When the boat departed with the jackal-headed oarsman, the dead
      man was here and gone.
Then the horrific was infused with beauty, and the dead man lit
      a lamp.
The dead man's ashen look is the dun result of his volatile
      condition.
The dead man loves you because your habits slay him, you tap your
      foot to the music, and your heart blows up when you gasp.

The Book of the Dead Man (#63)

1. About the Dead Man and Anyway

The dead man has up-the-stairs walking disorder.

He has one-foot-in-front-of-the-other indisposition and other
        aspects of the wistful.

He has over-the-hillitis, the past-one's-prime predicament of week-
        old celery or last year's universal theory.

The dead man has a pox, a condition, an affliction, the usual
        entropic timing, the sudden parsimony of a reformed
        spendthrift, all of it born of the purest, simplest love:
        gratitude for having been.

What if the dead man's love were less, would that make your
        pear wrinkle?

What if the dead man's truth were unsaid, would that cause you
        to kiss yourself down there?

Come on, come off it, be upstanding, it's not all fruits and
        vegetables, peaches and cream, rubber chickens or
        joy buzzers.

The dead man never said he wouldn't die.

Anyway, the dead man is too alive to have been dead all this time.

The dead man is the light that was turned on to study the dark.

Where there is no more nonetheless, no before or after, no
        henceforth or regardless, then the dead man in his
        infirmity, deformity, and prolonged ability overlaps his
        beloved in riotous whatchamacallit.

The dead man's language for love is largely blue-collar
        whatchamacallit.

2. More About the Dead Man and Anyway

The dead man rubs salt in his wound anyway.

When the dead man finds in himself a hollow, he fills it with
        salt anyway.

A little torture is breathtaking for as long as the dead man can
        hold his breath.

The discomfort that will not let the dead man sit still is transformed
        into curiosity by late-night abandon.

The beauty of the horrific is bled of its human cost by the long night
        of shaking.

The dead man, after long silence, sings his way through the
        graveyards.

If there is any way to change pigskin to silk, the dead man will
        find it.

Anyway, he has only one or two lives to give for his country.

He has only himself and his other self.

The dead man will not be countenanced or counterfeited, he will
        not be understood by the merely reasonable, he will not
        bleed his wounds of their hideous glamour and come
        up pristine.

Those who would slightly reorganize the bones will find their
        vanity unrewarded.

Those who would take the dead man's head away will lose
        themselves in the topography of his skull.

The dead man stands for what things are, not what you call them.

The dead man stands for living anyway.

The Book of the Dead Man (#65)

1. About the Dead Man and Sense

The dead man struggles not to become crabby, chronic or
        hypothetical.
He searches philosophy in vain for a pair of boots, a butterfly, a bent
        nail, an overlooked umbrella, some paste or scalp oil, but
        these new professors are all talk.
To the dead man, their theories are a kind of fretting, a way of
        blaming, a rightness carried to wrongheadedness, they
        have one another.
The dead man steps repeatedly into the stream, he does not wait for
        the water to be recycled.
His inclination is all downhill.
That's why the dead man likes all weather.
At bank's edge, he sees punk weed, tadpoles, pebbles that speak with
        mouths full of water, mud fit to be balm.
The water is less than it was to a fetus, but more than it will be.
How can the dead man explain water to these oversubscribed,
        arid phlegmatics?
A little water in the palm is worth the windpipes of a thousand tutors.
Helen Keller among these by-the-book tutors might still be waiting
        for a word.
Whitman's learned astronomer still prattles on about the distant
        stars, which for the dead man are at arm's reach.
The dead man laughs to see cold water thrown on language by those
        who are nourished by praise.
Their too many words have made a soupy alphabet.

2. *More About the Dead Man and Sense*

It would be wrong of the dead man to blame earth, water, fire or air.
It would be foolish to hold others hostage for a ransom that never
        existed.
It would be inescapably topsy-turvy to hold up to censure the
        material or the immaterial, the psychical or spiritual, the
        mental or emotional.
How curious now are the dead man's postures, struck in the dark
        for worms.
What on earth did the dead man imagine his frothiest words to
        be worth?
When there is no safe passage, no carriage wings, no golden ladder,
        no river to cross, no sage, no idiot, no ratchet wheel big
        enough or lever long enough then okay the dead man no
        longer strives to move the earth.
He would be one with missteps and failures, of a piece with error
        and fault, united with blemish and blunder.
He would be, and he is.
The dead man's thought is visceral and unconditional, love as it was
        intended when the river met the shore.

The Book of the Dead Man (#66)

1. About the Dead Man and Everpresence

That one was lost at sea and another to rot, that one threw himself
       from a roof and another from a bridge, and that he, of
       these and others, deferred and delayed has been a long
       astonishment to the dead man.
That he should be the green soul is a shock and a stupefaction.
To what end was it begotten that he be known among his late
       friends?
Why hath he not perished as studiously as prophecy foretold?
He has pals, but not so many now, who, borderlines, go their
       own ways.
When there is no more sacred or heretical, no promise, no guarantee,
       no warrant that places the millennium, no voltage too
       high or current too strong, then naturally there can be no
       one side, no one alone, no other and no otherwise.
Loam or grime, clay or dust, the dead man penetrates and
       permeates, he pervades and saturates and otherwise
       occupies every veneer, wrapper and facade.
Likewise, he hath gone dry in the leaves to better touch them.

2. More About the Dead Man and Everpresence

Shall the dead man doubt the axe or the envelope, the tar or the
        hinge, the birthday candle or the rubbery moon?
It is longer and longer that things are as they are.
Shall he ask the river to be a capsule, the shoesole to be a clockface,
        the library paste to be rivets?
The dead man knows that the owl's hoot is also a searchlight, that
        an enamel doorhandle may become a beacon, that milk is
        also bonemeal.
To be at all, the Whitmaniacal wonder of it, the Homeric — harsh
        register this age has come to, with all its data.
To be unknowing, through martial times or Chaucerian — soul-
        searing these days have been upon us.
The dead man leaves among the burned shirts, the shredded
        insulation, the free gases and syrups, amidst the upturned
        and rooted-out, hints of a trail made of basic materials.
Do not let them tell you that the dead man has gone on ahead.

The Book of the Dead Man (#68)

1. Accounts of the Dead Man

The dead man likes it when the soup simmers and the kettle hisses.

He wants to live as much as possible at the ends of his fingertips.

To make sense, to make nonsense, to make total sense, lasting sense,
ephemeral sense, giddy sense, perfect sense, holy sense.

The dead man wants it, he requires it, he trusts it.

Therefore, the dead man takes up with words as if they had nowhere
in mind.

The dead man's words are peacock feathers, bandages, all the
everyday exotica ground under by utility.

The dead man's book foresees a flickering awareness, an ember at
the end of the Void, a glitter, a glow beneath the ash.

The dead man's book is the radical document of time, nodding to
calamity and distress, happy in harm's way.

To the dead man, the mere whistling of a pedestrian may signal an
onslaught of intention.

The dead man calls his spillover a journal because it sounds helpless
and private, while a diary suggests the writings of
someone awaiting rescue.

The dead man doesn't keep a diary.

The dead man sweeps under the bed for scraps, pieces, chips,
tips, fringework, lace, filings and the rivets that rattled
and broke.

His is a flurry of nothing-more-to-give, the echo of a prolonged note
struck at the edge of an inverted bowl.

Now he must scrub his brain before a jury of his peers.

2. More Accounts of the Dead Man

The dead man has caused a consternation, but he didn't mean to.
He was just clocking his pulse, tracking his heart, feeling his way.
He was just dispersing the anomalous and otherwise scouting
       the self-evident and inalienable.
It was just that sometimes he couldn't stand it because he
       was happy.
It was the effect that he effected that affected him.
Some say it was his fervor for goose bumps took his breath away.
Some say it was the dead man's antsiness that put him in the dirt.
Some say he was too much the live wire, the living will, the holy
       spirit, the damn fool.
His was a great inhalation, wanton, a sudden swivel in the
       midst of struggle, a death dance with demons and
       other dagnabbits.
The dead man was well into physical geezerhood when he came to a
       conclusion and declared his independence.
At once he was chockablock with memories, the progeny of design
       and of blooper, boner and glitch.
He had his whole life to live.
When there is no more beseeching or gratitude, no seats remaining
       on the metaphysical seesaw, no zero-sum activity, no
       acquisition that is not also a loss, no finitude, then of
       course the dead man smiles as he blows a kiss through the
       wispy curtain of closure.
Some say the dead man was miserable to be so happy.

Index of Titles

Index of First Lines

About the Author

Marvin Bell is a distinguished poet and influential teacher who for the past thirty-five years has served as a faculty member at the Iowa Writers' Workshop. His many books of poetry and essays have earned him honors such as the Lamont Award of the Academy of American Poets, a nomination for the National Book Award in Poetry, fellowships from the Guggenheim Foundation and the National Endowment for the Arts, Senior Fulbrights to Yugoslavia and Australia, and an American Academy of Arts and Letters Award in Literature. In the year 2000 the State of Iowa made him its first Poet Laureate. Bell now teaches half the year in Iowa City. He apportions the rest of his time between Long Island, New York, and Port Townsend, Washington.

The Chinese character for poetry is made up of two parts: "word" and "temple."
It also serves as pressmark for Copper Canyon Press.

Founded in 1972, Copper Canyon Press remains dedicated to publishing
poetry exclusively, from Nobel laureates to new and emerging authors.
The Press thrives with the generous patronage of readers, writers,
booksellers, librarians, teachers, students, and funders—
everyone who shares the conviction that poetry invigorates the language
and sharpens our appreciation of the world.

PUBLISHER'S CIRCLE
The Allen Foundation for the Arts
Lannan Foundation
National Endowment for the Arts

EDITORS' CIRCLE
Thatcher Bailey
The Breneman Jaech Foundation
Cynthia Hartwig and Tom Booster
Port Townsend Paper Company
Target Stores
Emily Warn and Daj Oberg
Washington State Arts Commission

For information and catalogs:

COPPER CANYON PRESS
Post Office Box 271
Port Townsend, Washington 98368
360/385-4925
www.coppercanyonpress.org

Nightworks has been typeset for Copper Canyon Press at Stanton Publication Services, Inc., in Saint Paul, Minnesota. The typeface is Legacy, designed by Ron Arnholm. Legacy reinterprets Renaissance masterpieces for digital composition. The roman is based on a type cut in Venice by Nicolas Jenson around 1469. The italic is based on letters cut in Paris by Claude Garamond around 1539. This book was designed by Wendy Holdman and has been printed on acid-free paper by McNaughton & Gunn.